fore

ANGEL VISIONS II

Also by Doreen Virtue, Ph.D.

ANGEL VISIONS II

MORE TRUE STORIES OF PEOPLE WHO HAVE HAD
CONTACT WITH ANGELS, AND HOW YOU CAN, TOO!

DOREEN VIRTUE, PhD

HAY HOUSE

Australia • Canada • Hong Kong
South Africa • United Kingdom • United States

First published and distributed in the United Kingdom by:
Hay House UK Ltd, 292B Kensal Rd, London W10 5BE. Tel.: (44) 20 8962 1230;
Fax: (44) 20 8962 1239. www.hayhouse.co.uk

Published and distributed in the United States of America by:
Hay House, Inc., PO Box 5100, Carlsbad, CA 92018-5100. Tel.: (1) 760 431 7695 or
(800) 654 5126; Fax (1) 760 431 6948 or (800) 650 5115. www.hayhouse.com

Published and distributed in Australia by:
Hay House Australia Ltd, 18/36 Ralph St, Alexandra NSW 2015.
Tel.: (61) 2 9669 4299; Fax: (61) 2 9669 4144. www.hayhouse.com.au

Published and distributed in the Republic of South Africa by:
Hay House SA (Pty), Ltd, PO Box 990, Witkoppen 2068. Tel./Fax: (27) 11 706 6612.
orders@psdprom.co.za

Distributed in Canada by:
Raincoast, 9050 Shaughnessy St, Vancouver, BC V6P 6E5. Tel.: (1) 604 323 7100;
Fax: (1) 604 323 2600

The author of this book does not dispense medical advice or prescribe the use of any
technique as a form of treatment for physical or medical problems without the advice of
a physician, either directly or indirectly. The intent of the author is only to offer
information of a general nature to help you in your quest for emotional and spiritual
well-being. In the event you use any of the information in this book for yourself, which
is your constitutional right, the author and the publisher assume no responsibility for your
actions.

A catalogue record for this book is available from the British Library.

ISBN-10 1-4019-1065-5
ISBN-13 978-1-4019-1065-3

Editorial supervision: Jill Kramer
Design: Charles McStravick

Printed and bound in the UK by TJ International, Padstow, Cornwall.

To Archangel Michael

Contents

PREFACE

About Angel Visions

"**W**hy are so many people having angel encounters these days?" the reporter asked me. Her question was one that I heard frequently.

"I don't claim to know all the answers," I told her. "But I do ask a lot of questions, and I'm very satisfied with the answers I've received from my meditations, my interviews with clients and workshop attendees, and my scientific research.

"Our prayers for guidance and protection have been answered," I explained, "by God sending additional angels to our side. Angels have always been with us, but more of them are now here among us because of our prayers.

"The millennium had a lot to do with it. Many people became frightened as 1999 drew to a close, and they prayed hard for protection. Their fears about Y2K and an apocalypse triggered a new spiritual renaissance.

"The angels aren't only triggered by our prayers; they're also sent to us purposely at this time of *great spiritual awakening*. They're here as our teachers, helping us to appreciate the Divine love within ourselves and each other."

"Does *everyone* have angels?" the reporter asked. Her question implied that some people might not deserve guardian angels.

"Oh, yes," I replied. *"Everyone* has angels. It's just that some people don't *listen* to their angels. But those angels are always standing by, unconditionally loving the human to whom they're assigned, and awaiting that person's prayers for assistance."

"And can anyone talk with their angels?" This question often comes from people who were taught that only high-level members of organized religions, or gifted psychics, can talk to heaven.

"God and our angels talk to us constantly, and we do hear them, even if we attribute their messages to intuition or coincidence," I answered. "Science shows that everyone has the capacity for telepathy or mind-to-mind communication. It's no more difficult to use our telepathic mind to talk with the angels than it is to tune in to who's calling when the telephone rings."

The reporter's questions mirrored the inquiries that I frequently receive at my workshops. People ask about the nature of heaven, life-after-death, and the angelic realm. I'm so happy about our collective openness to spirituality! Many of us are answering a deep inner calling to help the angels on an Earthly level.

The stories that you'll read in *Angel Visions II* offer additional insight into the afterlife and the angelic realm. For instance, the stories in Chapter 3: "Near-Death Experience Visions," emphasize that we won't die unless it's our time to go. The descriptions of deceased loved ones in Chapters 2, 4, and 12 show that most people in heaven are happy, are free of their burdensome bodies, and feel undying love for us. And Chapters 1, 9, and 11 reveal that we're eternally being watched over and protected.

You'll probably find that the synchronicities in your life increase while you're reading this book. By focusing upon angel experiences, you tend to have more of them. I certainly noticed an increase while I was editing the stories in this book. For instance, I edited the story called "Protected from a Tornado" in Chapter 8 while on an airplane headed toward the Minneapolis airport. As I read Judy Mitchell's description of the green sky that precipitated the tornado, I thought that she surely must have been mistaken.

Then, 30 minutes later, we landed at the airport. We noticed many people gathered at the windows, intently staring at the sky. Although it was only 4:30 P.M., the sky was nearly dark. Something was wrong! Then, a remarkable thing happened: The sky grew black, and then it turned the darkest, most putrid shade of green I'd ever seen. The first time I'd heard about a green sky had only been a half hour earlier, and now I was experiencing it firsthand! The airport ceased all flights in and out due to tornados in the surrounding areas. Our airport was hit by enormous hail and winds, and it was several hours before we could fly to our destination.

The second amazing synchronicity connected to this book occurred while I edited "A Call from My Angel" in Chapter 6. Suzanne Goodnough wrote that she heard her guardian angel introduce himself to her as "Maurice." Suzanne was unsure of this name, though, and asked for validation, which she received in a most humorous way (as you'll read about in the story). I was on a train while editing the story, and twice looked up to see large building signs that read "Maurice."

In the first *Angel Visions* book, I emphasized *seeing* the angelic realm. I find that most people who attend my workshops request that I teach them clairvoyance skills. Even though we *can* connect with angels through nonvisual ways, such as voices, feelings, and thoughts, most of my audience members want to *see* the angels. In that book, I included step-by-step instructions for opening up one's clairvoyance for angel visions.

Many people wrote me letters saying that they'd experienced angel visions and encounters by following the instructions in the book. Several of their stories are included in this sequel. You'll learn what triggered other people's angel encounters so that you can apply these methods yourself.

In *Angel Visions II*, you'll also see how angel encounters affect the people involved. For instance, those who are grieving are emotionally healed as a result of their dreamtime or apparition visits with deceased loved ones. Far from being a gruesome meeting with a zombie, as Hollywood portrays the dead, these visitations are love-filled, moving reunions. The deceased loved one reassures the living by saying, "I'm fine. Don't worry about me. Please go on with your life, enjoy yourself, and make a positive difference in the world."

Many of the stories in this book discuss lifesaving angel encounters, such as a voice warning someone of danger in the nick of time. Other stories show how angels helped people love themselves more and be kinder to others. Still others illustrate the great sense of humor that God, the angels, and our deceased loved ones possess.

You'll see how heaven watches over us, protecting us from harm by giving us warnings and assistance. In Chapter 5, you'll read about strangers who appeared from out of nowhere and gave solace or assistance, and then disappeared without a trace. Chapter 10 is filled with dramatic stories about disembodied voices that saved people's lives. Since my own life was saved (and forever changed) by hearing a voice before and during an armed carjacking in 1995, this chapter is especially meaningful to me.

In Part II, you'll learn the methods that I teach in my psychic-development workshops to awaken our natural spiritual gifts. Be assured that you *do* have angels and guides with you right now who are already in contact with you. The methods in this book can bring your relationship with heaven to a more conscious level so you're more aware of who's around you in the spirit world.

The power of God and the angels is unlimited. If we will just hold the intention of connecting with them, they will do all of the work. *That's* how much they love us!

Acknowledgments

My gratitude to all of the angelic people who allowed me to print their stories so that we all may benefit. Because of your willingness to openly share your angel experiences, we are all enriched. Thank you! Angel blessings to Jill Kramer, Reid Tracy, Louise L. Hay, Ron Tillinghast, Corcy Wolfe, Bronny Daniels, and Jill Wellington Schaeff.

>€ >€ >€

PART I

*True Stories of People
Who Have Seen Angels**

*Author's Note: Certain individuals have requested that
only their first name or initials be used to identify them.

CHAPTER ONE

Angel Visions

A Visit from Gabriel
by Jessica Dickson

When I was about seven years old, I was awakened by the feeling of a presence, and a voice calling my name softly. I looked around but didn't see anything. I heard my name called again. Rubbing my eyes, I strained to look through the darkness. I looked out my doorway into the hall.

My mother always left the door cracked open a little and kept the light on for me. Tonight the light was different. It was so bright white that I couldn't look directly at it. Still scanning, my eyes started to distinguish amazingly brilliant whites and golds and softer shades of white.

A shape started to form, but not a solid shape. It was immensely tall. It had wings that were so huge that they weren't entirely visible to me. I know they went way up beyond the figure's head and the ceiling. The wings were like long, feathered fingers of light, airy, and transparent soft white light. Even in a resting position, they were enormous, almost touching the ground, and they didn't fold completely down, but remained slightly fanned.

The being's feet bore the most unusual sandals I'd ever seen. They were like thick pieces of wood or leather and secured by straps that went up to "his" ankles. He was dressed in a robe that was flowing and white, and it was belted around the waist by a gold cord. Above his head hovered a ring of bright golden light, and when he bowed his head down, it would disappear, and all I could see was blazing white light and the golden glow that surrounded his body. He had long, wavy golden hair that rested on his broad shoulders, and his eyes were piercing and ice blue. He said that his name was Gabriel.

I couldn't believe what I was seeing. I looked away and became very frightened. I tried to scream for my mother, but my voice wouldn't work. I couldn't cry out. I looked back toward the closet, hoping it was my imagination and that it was just the light playing tricks on me. He had not gone away, and my fear increased tenfold. He told me, "Be not afraid." I immediately became filled with love and warmth, and my fear subsided.

I listened while he spoke. Actually, "spoke" is an incorrect description. Angels don't speak like you and I do. They communicate with thoughts and emotions, with peace and love, from their crown to yours. They fill you with such peace and love that you'll be warm all over, from the inside out. They radiate a brilliant aura of light in white and gold. They're so radiant that they're luminous. The white layer is so intense that it's almost blinding. Angels impart a feeling of great strength and power, but in the same instance, they're gentle and loving beyond what we can experience here.

It's unconditional love at its purest—free of judgment regardless of our circumstances or our sins. Gabriel continued to communicate with me. His thoughts were burned into my memory as single words and flashes of intense emotion. Gabriel stopped briefly to ask if I understood, or if I accepted. I remember nodding in awe, feeling intense responsibility and purpose and becoming more spiritually aware than my Earth years would dictate. I only remembered bits and pieces of our conversation.

Gabriel told me that my life would be hard and I would lose my faith, but God would never leave me and I would find my way back. The angel imparted the sense of God's immense love and happiness for me and the knowledge that we would all be reunited. Even at such a young age, I knew that I was agreeing to serve God, even knowing that it wouldn't be easy. I had to be willing to sacrifice my will and my life when and if it was commanded, and perhaps deal with being ridiculed by others because I wouldn't be understood, much less believed.

Without a word, the brightness began to dim, and I watched Gabriel ascend through the roof. His bottom half was visible in my world, and his top half, where my ceiling began, was invisible. I blinked in disbelief, and he vanished.

As I grew up, I remembered more of Gabriel's visit, and it made more sense to me. I also had other encounters—the angels appearing as blinding white and gold light with little stars or bright specks suspended in it, surrounding me with the same warmth and love.

Do you want to know how you can meet your angels? Open up your heart. Be true. Be still, and you will find them, for they're always nearby, waiting for us to believe in them.

❀❀❀

Meeting My Angel
by Terri Sanderson

About three years ago, I was going through a really tough time, and I was very depressed. I didn't care about life, and I had already made two suicide attempts. One night, I was awakened by someone who was sitting at the end of my bed—I lived alone at the time! I sat up and saw my angel sitting there. He had long brown hair and was wearing a white gown. For some reason, the sight of him frightened me, so I pulled the covers up over my head. My heart was pounding.

But then I heard him say, "Don't worry. I am not here to hurt you. I am here to protect you." Since that time, I have felt less afraid and depressed.

꿀꿀꿀

Feeling Safe Again
by Greta Guldemont

I was a victim of a brutal rape. My unknown attacker broke into my apartment late at night while I was sleeping. Two years later, even though I had moved out of state and was living with my husband, I suffered from terrible nightmares where bad people were chasing me and trying to hurt me. I would awake exhausted nearly every morning.

One night before Christmas, I had watched the movie *Miracle on 34th Street,* and later I was having a dream about the movie when I heard a voice ask me, "Are you all right?" It was a man's voice, and his words filled my body with an incredible warmth and peacefulness. I opened my eyes and saw a figure of a man at the foot of our bed. (My husband was sleeping beside me.)

Ordinarily, the sight of a strange man in my bedroom probably would have filled me with terror (as a result of my rape experience). But I just lay there, as peaceful and happy as could be, still enjoying the feeling of warmth throughout my body. He repeated his words, asking me if I was all right, and again I felt that incredible warmth through my body as I said yes.

He said that he was watching over me, and I remember smiling and then drifting off into the most wonderful deep, healing sleep. Was my heavenly visitor an angel, or was he the spirit of my dad who died when I was a baby? Regardless, I had *no* more nightmares after that! I've been so grateful for this experience.

❧❧❧

The Room Is Full of Angels
by Enid Haban-Megahed

On December 28, 2000, I was just waking up, my mind thinking of things before I got out of bed. It had been a difficult holiday season. I had lost my son three years earlier, and his birthday had been two days before Christmas.

Suddenly, the room was filled with light. As I looked to the left, I saw angels; as I turned around, the room was *filled* with angels. I was amazed. As I slowly turned around, I was surrounded by angels and bright light. When I completed the circle, I was in front of a huge ten-foot angel who didn't have a distinct form like all the other angels around me. I reached out and up to the big angel. Three times I asked to go with them, but he said that I couldn't go yet. They needed my intellect and my strength here on Earth.

They held me. When I turned to look again, the white light was gone, and the room was normal. I was in shock for a week before I could even tell anyone about the visit and message.

❧❧❧

Never Alone
by Suzanne B.

Several months ago, I was very discouraged and down about life. My son was seriously ill, I was having problems at work, and I also felt hurt due to a good friend's actions. I went to sleep very upset with all these things on my mind, and I prayed for God and my angels to help me.

Around 3:00 A.M., I felt that someone (other than my husband) was in bed beside me. I felt a little scared, but I turned around. I saw a large form lying beside me, and I could see the outline of feathers of the angel's wing. There was also a green hue toward the edge of the wing's profile. I turned back and fell asleep, feeling very comforted that I am never alone in both my joyful and sad times.

My Comforting Angel
by Tamar Goldbery

I was crying myself to sleep one night, as I was really distressed over a failed relationship. I was sobbing, practically shaking, when I felt the presence of a lady sitting beside me on my bed near my pillow.

As she began stroking my hair, I felt an instant calm and fell asleep. But I saw her. She had long white hair and appeared to be in her 60s. From that day on, I have never felt alone, and I know that there's always someone with me.

Angelica
by Charles F. Turpin

One Friday night at my job, I had to walk up six flights of stairs to a small protected area where I work with machinery. Out of the blue, I felt a sharp pain in my chest, so I lay my head down on my desk. But the pain grew until it was hurting a lot. I tried calling my co-worker downstairs for help, but he didn't answer.

Then I happened to look out the window and saw a person— a woman. She didn't look like anything I had seen in church or a movie. I will never forget what she looked like. She was outside the window of my work area, 60 feet above the ground!

Her eyes were sparkling blue—not like any blue you could paint, and not like anything in a science fiction movie, but beautiful. She didn't have a robe on, like the kind you always picture on angels. She was naked. But her skin was as white as I had ever seen—so white that the details of her body were hidden.

Her hair was red, long, and fluttering as her wings slowly flapped. Her wings weren't like a dove's, but more like a sparrow's.

She never said hello, and she never had a glow around her, like in the movies. She was a real live being or soul. I tried to raise my head, but she came to me and laid her hand on my head and turned my neck to where I could see her better. She just looked at me. She didn't speak through her lips, but through her mind. She said, "It isn't time yet." Then for some reason, I just happened to ask her, "What's your name?" and she said, "Angelica."

It seemed like I blinked my eyes, and then it was time to go. I drove myself home, and my wife took me to the hospital. The tests showed that I'd had a heart attack that evening.

But they did another test the following Monday, and it showed that my heart was miraculously undamaged. Since then, I've also survived cancer—even though I only had a 10 percent chance of living. Somehow I feel that Angelica is still around, helping me to survive.

❦❦❦

"Look, It's an Angel!"
by Ann Reiff

I had a dream that my two sisters and I were in the kitchen and an angel appeared. He was male, very large, fair-skinned, and had wavy blond hair to his shoulders. His wingspan was about three feet on each side. I said to my sisters in surprise, "Look, it's an angel!" I made a comment to them in my dream that I wasn't even afraid. I woke up, and it felt so real.

A week later, my siblings and I received word that my mother had been diagnosed with cancer and that she had been taken to the hospital. My sister from Australia and my other sister and I flew to California to be with my mother. We all stayed at my mother's house.

As my sisters and I stood together in my mother's bathroom, I felt such a sense of déjà vu. The scene was identical to the one in my dream! Given the great distance that my sisters and I lived from one another, the odds of us being all together were quite slim. I knew that my dream was a message from my angel letting me know that my mother was ill but that she would be okay. Today, years later, my mother is doing great.

❦❦❦

My Life's-Purpose Angel
by Pia Wilson

I had been meditating and trying some automatic writing to get to know my guardian angels better. I learned that the angel helping me fulfill my life purpose was named Jim. At the time, I was feeling that my ambitions wouldn't amount to anything, and I was very frustrated. I accused Jim of not working hard enough on my behalf.

That night, I had a dream. It was one of those dreams that feels more than real. In it, I was talking to a human friend of mine, whose name is also Jim. I was joking with him, the way I normally would in life, but he wasn't responding appropriately. I got angry with him, then I noticed something. His eyes were quite different. And although on the surface he looked like my human friend, Jim, he was actually someone else. His eyes were wider and took up more of his face, and his cheekbones were particularly high.

I realized that this was my angel Jim, which explained the lack of humor. Through my meditations and automatic writing, I've come to know that Angel Jim is very serious. He took me to a room where there were hundreds of "people" sitting at computer terminals. Jim was showing me how many angels were working with him to help me fulfill my life purpose.

Jim has continued to appear to me in my dreams around the periods in the last few months when I've made strides in my career. I always feel especially good after a dream involving him, and he's even led the way for my romance angel to use my dreams to communicate with me. Angels are wonderful for love, guidance, and advice. I can't imagine life without them now.

❦❦❦

The Angel Who Tucked Me In
by Angie Chiste

In 1986, when I was 18, I got a job as a waitress at an all-night truck stop located in a small Canadian hamlet, far away from my family. Our staff accommodations consisted of an old hotel. We each had our own room, with doors that locked automatically when you closed them, like most hotel rooms.

One morning, I got off work at 6:00 A.M. after working all night. I went to my room to get some sleep. I was so tired that I lay down on my bed, still in my uniform, without taking my shoes off. Sometime later, I awoke to the feeling of my shoes being taken off. I lifted my head and saw a transparent lady engulfed in light. She took off my shoes and gently covered me with a blanket. I lay back and knew she would watch over me while I slept. I wasn't scared at all.

When I awoke, I was under the covers, my shoes neatly in the corner. I knew no one came into my room, as the doors automatically locked when I entered my room. It was an angel taking care of me after a long day's work.

The Day I Saw the Angels
by Laura Weintraub

It was a usual Tuesday morning, and I was getting the kids ready for school. My son Aaron was the sleepy bear of the family, and I always had difficulty dragging him out of bed. Aaron is always the first to get my attention because he starts school an hour before my other son, Alexander.

By the time that Aaron got downstairs on this particular morning, he barely had ten minutes for breakfast. Mornings have always been tough for him; it's as if he's dragging a boulder behind him. To top it off, Aaron started in on Alexander, teasing him and irritating him.

I had recently been studying *A Course in Miracles*, and I was learning a lot about myself and others. I watched how my children constantly provoked one another, always trying to best the other. I started to talk to Aaron, asking him why he was teasing Alexander. It was as if Aaron was taking his frustrations out on him! Aaron started to tell me about school and how he felt that the other kids didn't like him. I've found that when one of my kids is feeling hurt inside, they have a tendency to take it out on each other, so I tried to help him see what might be causing the problem.

Just then, my husband stormed into the kitchen, and he snapped at me to hurry up and get Aaron to school. I immediately felt like I was being attacked, and I allowed myself to feel hurt. I went to my room and cried. Then it dawned on me that I was *choosing* to feel attacked and to get my feelings hurt. If I chose to perceive my husband's actions differently, I could have a different outcome. I realized that I could change my perceptions anytime I wanted. It took me a couple of hours to forgive my husband and let go, but I did because I didn't want to feel this way the rest of the day.

I started to pray and meditate. I asked God to bring peace to me and my family, and to help me forgive my husband, my kids, and most of all, myself. I had to let go and allow them to learn their lessons on their own, trusting that God and the angels were with them, too! I no longer needed to feel that I had to be in control of everything.

As I sat and prayed in my room, I suddenly heard a tap on the window. I thought it was a bird or something. To my amazement, though, I saw that the sky was filled with angels! They were everywhere. I started to cry with joy. I truly wanted to see angels, and I really didn't know when or where it was going to happen. I realized that I had to be completely free and clear from all attack thoughts in order to experience their presence. I realized that they are all around us in everything we see, and that we are all one!

That afternoon, Alexander and I stopped at the drive-through to get an after-school snack. I was singing a song on the radio when my son said, "Mom, there's a face looking at me!" as he pointed his finger to the sky. "Is that an angel?" he asked. As I sat in amazement, Alexander exclaimed, "And there's another, and another!"

"Yes!" I agreed, as tears rolled down my face. It was a miracle. He was seeing exactly what I saw earlier that day.

Alexander was so excited and said, "I can't wait to tell Aaron. But what if he doesn't believe me?" I told him not to worry, and I said a little prayer, "Please, Aaron, don't tease him this time!"

As soon as we got home, Alexander raced up the stairs to tell his brother. I heard him say, "Aaron, guess what? I saw an angel looking at me, and then I saw three more!"

Then Aaron gently patted him on the back and he simply said, "That's cool, man!" I smiled, tears running down my face, as they gave each other a big hug.

That was a special day—one I will always remember. It was the day I saw the angels! From that day on, I was constantly aware of their presence; Divine love; and protection for me, my family, and all of us.

◆◆◆◆

Comfort from Home
by G. G.

When I was very little, I had a very vivid dream. In it, I saw myself standing, suspended in a dark blue sky. Around me were five or more beings, dressed in hooded capes and dresses. I couldn't see their faces, yet I knew in some way that I was one of them. I can't find the words to describe the unconditional love I received from this group of beings. I had nothing to explain, nothing to prove. They loved me the way I was.

I spoke with them in a telepathic way. I said I wanted to go back to Earth. They answered, "You don't have to go." But I repeated my desire. They said, "It will be harsh and difficult." But I said that I wanted to go back anyway. They didn't interfere. I then saw myself dive downward and return to life on Earth.

My guides were right; my childhood *was* difficult. I was the eldest daughter of eight children, and I often felt that I had to deal with my problems all by myself. In moments of loneliness, I'd think of my angel guides and their love, and I'd instantly muster up the courage to go on with my life.

ЭЄ ЭЄ ЭЄ

CHAPTER TWO

Apparition Visions

"She'll Wait for You"
by Kimberly Miller

It was December of 1986, three months after my father died, and my mother was in the hospital for heart failure. I had promised my dad while he was dying that I would look after my mom even though our relationship was very strained.

While visiting my mother one afternoon, I realized that I could smell my father's cologne. I checked each of my brothers, thinking that they were wearing it, but none of them were. I was the only one who could smell the cologne. I went back into the room and felt a presence on the left-hand side of my mother's hospital bed, and again I could smell my father's favorite cologne. I knew then that he was there watching over my mother and waiting for her.

That evening after leaving the hospital to visit my mom, I went home to string Christmas-tree lights for my kids. I received a call from the hospital to get there as soon as possible because my mom had taken a turn for the worse. I hopped into my car, doing well over the speed limit to get to the hospital.

As I was racing along, a sudden chill came over me, and I glanced at the passenger seat to see my father sitting there.

All he said was, "She'll wait for you; you need to slow down," and then he was gone.

❀❀❀

Bless His Heart
by Dianne Galligan

Fourteen years ago, I lost my younger brother (age 29) to suicide. When I got home on the day of his funeral, my answering-machine tape had all been used up. Yet everyone who knew me knew that I was at my brother's funeral. I played the tape, and all I heard was an electrical sound throughout the whole tape. I knew that it was my brother communicating with me. He used to call and tease me on my answering machine all the time.

A month later, my father had a massive heart attack. My brother appeared to me (I know I wasn't sleeping!) and told me he was coming to get my dad. I begged my brother not to take my father because this was only a month after his (my brother's) death. I told him that we needed Dad, and my mother couldn't possibly handle another death so soon. So I prayed to God and sent angels to my father to protect him. I called the hospital, and they told me that my dad was having a very bad night.

I know it was the angels that helped Dad stay with us for another eight years even though his heart was very bad. When Dad died in 1994, the doctors said they didn't know how he had lived so long because his heart was so damaged. But I knew why!

❀❀❀

Angel Baby
by Suzanna Lonchar

The little fat baby had just given me another one of his adorable smiles. I was about 11 years old at the time and often stopped by to play with him at a neighbor's house about three doors down the street. The infant was nicknamed Baby Butch, and I was taken by his charming smile and good nature. He was about nine months old, a beautiful baby with a head full of thick auburn curls.

The children's mother, whom I will name "Nora," was desperate to go out one evening, but she couldn't find a baby-sitter. She asked my mother if I could baby-sit, but my mother said that I was too young for the responsibility.

Later that evening, I awakened from a deep sleep to see the most beautiful vision I'd ever seen. Baby Butch was floating by the foot of my bed surrounded in clouds. The vision was so brilliant that it illuminated the room. Baby Butch was wearing a crown, and it looked like he was surrounded by diamonds, rubies, and jewels sparkling all around him like angel lights. He was gurgling, laughing, and happy. He had little wings and wore a little robe in a brilliant red velvet. It was the most magnificent sight! He resembled a picture of baby Jesus I had seen, with his tight auburn curls. The vision may have only lasted for a few seconds, but it was real, my eyes were wide open, and this was no dream. Afterwards, I must have drifted back into a deep sleep.

In the early hours of the morning, I was suddenly awakened by someone hysterically banging on our front door. I jumped out of bed and rushed downstairs. It was our next-door neighbor hysterically screaming, "Baby Butch is dead! Baby Butch is dead!"

It was six o'clock in the morning, and Nora had just come home after leaving her children alone for the night. When she looked in the baby's crib, she discovered that he was dead. It appeared that he had strangled or smothered, for he had somehow twisted the bedsheets around his neck.

Baby Butch visited me that night to show me that he was now an angel. He was giving me the message to not grieve because he was with Jesus. Since that time, I have known that death is not final, there *is* a heaven, and angels are real.

❦❦❦

My Angel Daughter
by Mary Anne Luppino

In 1987, I was four months pregnant with my first child. During the night, I suddenly woke up and saw a small female child-spirit standing at the bottom corner of my side of the bed. She walked up to stand in front of my face, and I automatically, without knowing what I was doing, reached out to hold her. Then she disappeared. I realized after my child was born (I was sure I was going to have a boy but instead had a girl) that the spirit I saw was my daughter, Luciana, and it was at that moment that her spirit entered the fetus. I know that sounds strange, but I feel strongly that it's true.

)€)€)€

CHAPTER THREE

Near-Death Experience Visions

What I Saw in Heaven
by Jeannene Bethea

It was Saturday night, March 13, 1999, at 11:30 P.M. My husband gave me a good-night kiss, told me he loved me, and we went to sleep. The next morning, my husband recalls that when he woke up, I was sitting on the side of the bed acting peculiarly. He said he asked me, "Are you okay, honey?"

My answer was, "I am doing my exercises." He said that I had my arms up in the air acting like a monkey. Then he said I told him that I felt funny and was going back to sleep, so he decided to do the same. But within 30 minutes, something woke him up. My husband is a very heavy sleeper, so it must have been angels who woke him. He called my name and I would not respond, so he reached over and touched me because he said I looked so white. He said I was very cold and clammy, and it frightened him.

He then called out for our 17-year-old daughter's help. They tried to dress me to take me to the hospital, but he said I was like a limp dishrag and they couldn't get me dressed, so they called an ambulance. As soon as the paramedics arrived, they put me on a life-support system.

I was taken to the hospital, and within an hour, my husband was called into the Intensive Care Unit and was informed of my diagnosis: My kidneys had completely failed. That, in turn, had caused all my other organs to shut down. My condition looked bad, and the doctor advised my husband to gather family members to my bedside to say their final good-byes. My husband then had to tell our three daughters, ages 22, 17, and 10, that their mother might not make it.

Unaware of what was happening, I was in the process of going through a tunnel of white light to the most beautiful, peaceful, and unbelievable place you can ever imagine. Everything was so clear, so white, and so pure. I felt at home.

Angels were everywhere, each in their own glass ball, just floating around! I had no glass ball, but I was floating, too. I felt as if I couldn't keep my balance. I was going backwards, then forward, then up, then down. But each time I started to fall, an angel would come out of a ball and help me stand up straight so I wouldn't hurt myself. They were there to protect me.

There were also different-colored poles. I didn't understand their meaning then or now, unless they represented the rainbow of heaven. I'm still not sure about this.

While all of this was happening, I heard a voice say, "It's time for her to go home, angels." This voice was so clear, yet so strong. "It is not her time yet, and she does not deserve to come here this way." Then the voice was gone.

Two of the angels came out of their glass balls and brought me back through yet another white-light tunnel until I was home. They guided me to open my eyes and, of course, I didn't know where I was or what had happened. When I awoke, it was nearly a week after I'd been checked into the hospital. My husband and brother were standing beside my bed looking frightened.

During my week's stay in the hospital, I had five kidney dialysis treatments while I was unconscious. After I regained consciousness, I had a sixth dialysis treatment and was told that I would require them three times weekly, perhaps forever. Miraculously, though, I have never had another treatment, and everything went back to normal by March 22, 1999.

The doctors have never found out why this happened to me, what caused it, or why I'm still here, but *I* know why I'm still here: God. The doctors call me their miracle woman.

To be sent to a place of such joy, peace, and beauty that no dream could ever touch, or words could ever describe; with no secrets, and with everything in full view with nothing hidden, is something I can never explain to anyone. We do not have these words in the dictionary, only in our hearts.

Why give me a taste of cake and take it away? I asked for months afterward, and finally I heard the answer from God Himself: "I am God. I am your Creator; I wrote the book before you were born. Everything is in Divine order. You have to fulfill the will I have written for you, and then you can come home. So for now, love with all your heart, and spread your light wherever you go, or whatever you do, this I ask of you."

Now, each day, I wait for His lessons to teach me His way.

◊◊◊

My Reunion with Dad
by Shirley Finch

My father lived in Idaho, and I lived in California. Dad called me late one night in April of 1979. He was crying, and he pleaded with me to bring my two little girls and come visit him before it was too late.

I said, "Oh, Dad, I'll be there in June when the girls get out of school."

He said, "It will be too late."

I talked with my dad for a while, and he kept on begging me to come. I asked if he was sick, and he said he wasn't, but he just knew that it would be too late.

One month later, my sister called me with the terrible news of Dad's death. My father passed away in a horrible auto accident while hunting with my two older brothers. I was stunned, and my phone conversation with Dad kept replaying in my mind. I was sick about it, and I chastised myself for not going.

My mother told me that, prior to the accident, Dad had been getting his things in order because he knew it was "his time." My mother thought he was crazy to say such a thing. My brothers said that the night before the accident, Dad had told them, "If I go tonight, I just want you to know how much I love you." Hours later, he was dead.

In June of 1986, I was shot with a .38 semi-automatic weapon. The bullet went through my left arm, and on through my lung, and then it lodged in my spine. I "died" in the ambulance. The paramedics gave me CPR and a shot of adrenalin through the heart.

While I was gone, I was traveling in this very dark space. I'm not sure if I was traveling up, down, sideways, or where. There was a little light. The closer I got, the bigger the light got. When I reached it, my dad was standing in the light. I was standing in the dark, getting ready to walk toward him because I was so happy to see him. I missed him so much!

Then he said, "You're not supposed to be here now."

I said, "That's okay. I'm happy to see you." I wanted so badly to go to him and give him a hug, but my foot wouldn't budge. I could not step into the light.

In a stern voice, my dad said, "No! Go home. Your kids need you." At that moment, I opened my eyes, and my mother was in the emergency room holding my hand. My experiences have changed me forever. Now, I live every day as if it were my last. I still make plans and have goals to look forward to, but I make an extra effort to be nice to everybody. I tell my family and friends that I love them and that I always will. And I help strangers in need. I have developed a caring heart, thanks to my experiences.

❦❦❦

It Wasn't My Time Yet
by Brenda J. Salazar

One morning in July of 2000, my grandson Brandon tried to wake me up to get him some milk. When I wouldn't wake up, he got my youngest daughter, Eva. But Eva couldn't wake me up either. Panicked, Eva called an ambulance. The paramedics couldn't revive me even though they tried smelling salts and a sternum rub.

While all of this was going on around me, I was having an adventure of my own! The bright light that's so associated with near-death experiences was there. I saw my Grandma and Grandpa Beggs. My stepdad was also there, holding my little godchild, Tianna Marie, who had died as a stillborn baby. My husband's father and grandparents were there, too. I had never met his grandparents, as they had died years before. There were great-aunts and uncles that I knew, and some whom I didn't know.

All of these relatives wanted me to give messages to different people. The whole time I was communicating with these relatives, my Grandma Beggs was telling me, "Go back, you aren't supposed to be here. Hurry, go back!"

The next thing I remember is telling the paramedics to watch out for my back! They were taking me down the stairs of my apartment in some sort of chair contraption and hitting each step very hard. I believe my grandmother pushed me back into my body. I gave everyone the messages that I'd been asked to deliver to them and told them about my experience. I described my husband's grandparents to a T, which amazed my mother-in-law, since I hadn't even been born when they had crossed over.

ʙʙʙ

Chapter Four

Dream Visitations
from Deceased Loved Ones

"No, Don't Cry"
by Jeanine Beny

My father, to whom I was very close, passed away on April 15, 1987, when I was 19 years old. I was absolutely devastated because of the suddenness, and also because I hadn't been there when he died. He was diagnosed with cancer, and one week later, my father was dead.

I finally received some peace of mind about one month later on Mother's Day, when I had a visit from my dad during a dream. In it, I was cleaning the inside of my car. I looked up and saw my father walking toward me, dressed in the same navy uniform that we had buried him in. He came right to the door of the car, and I stood up and started crying.

Dad shook his head, as if to say, "No, don't cry." I asked him if he knew how much I loved him. He nodded a "Yes" to me. Again, I started crying and told him how much I missed him and how much I loved him. I then asked him if he was out of pain and happy, and he again nodded a "Yes."

Then he took my hand in his hand and rubbed it against my cheek. To this day, I can still remember how that felt. He then looked at me as if to say, "I have to go," and walked across the street onto my neighbor's lawn and disappeared. I woke up in a cold sweat, but somehow had a newfound sense of ease about his death.

I hope my story helps someone else as much as my dad's visit helped me.

❦❦❦

Dad Is Still with Us
by Michelle Massip Handel

My father died suddenly of a heart attack at age 61. My mother, brother, and I were shocked. One night after his death, I had an auditory experience where he told me to stop making such a big deal out of it, that he was fine, and that he didn't want me to feel so sad. I called my mother immediately, only to find out that she'd had a similar experience.

My brother was at the beach at the time, and when he returned home, he called me. He said, "I just want you to know that I was down at the beach thinking about Dad, and he's okay." Then I told him about my mother and my own similar experience.

The three of us continued to have dream visitations. When I woke up from one of these dream visits, I felt as if I had spent time with my dad in every sense of the word. It felt very good. Dad and I visited in my dreams the nights before my birthday for several years. I felt like it was my birthday gift from him.

One day, my mother told me that she broke down crying because she couldn't fix something in the house, something my father would have taken care of. She heard him tell her to get a tool out in the garage, and he even told her specifically where it was.

I'm no longer getting visits from my father in my dreams that I remember, but I certainly talk to him and feel his presence.

❦❦❦

Dad's Reassurance
by Carol W.

My father lived alone in Arizona, quite a distance from his other family members and me. My sisters and I spoke with him by phone regularly, so when we didn't hear from him for several days, we got worried. My sister called the local police and requested that they go to Dad's home. They found my father dead on his bed. Apparently he had died several days earlier.

An autopsy was never conducted, as the coroner said that Dad died of natural causes. However, it bothered my sisters and me that we never found out what our father died of.

Over the next few months, I would wake up out of a sound sleep with the feeling of my father's presence at the end of my bed. But I was too afraid to look at his apparition in case he looked frighteningly decayed, like when his body was discovered by the police. I shared this fear with my sister, and she reassured me that Dad would look just like he did when he was healthy and living.

Well, my sister was right. I had a dream where she and I were putting dishes away and talking about Dad. The next thing I remember, everything turned white around me. My sister was no longer there, and my dad was sitting at my kitchen table. I remember how good he looked, and I told him so. I also told him that I loved him and missed him. I noticed that while sitting there, he wasn't smoking or drinking coffee like he always did. I also asked him what happened. He told me that he died of a heart attack. After that, I woke up and have been at peace about my father ever since.

❧❧❧❧

Divine Message from Dad
by Judith Waite

My father, Colin, died in 1987 from a heart attack and also hardening of the arteries. This condition was caused by his two vices, drinking beer and smoking. He would say these two habits "never hurt anyone but himself" . . . how untrue. When someone dies unexpectedly, the family is devastated.

My father was not a religious or spiritual man, and I only knew of him going to church at funerals, weddings, and baptisms. But my father came in dream form to me several times and was much more spiritually knowledgeable than he had appeared in Earthly form. He spoke to me about being there to help Mum and also to help me with personal problems. When I woke up, I could still feel the warmth of his hand holding mine.

Sometime later, I heard my father speak to me. I was astounded by how spiritually wise he was. He said, "There is no 'early,' mistimed death. It is all worked to plan—not God's plan, as such—but each individual as they come to Earthly life also chooses their time of departure. No baby is born without this understanding.

"We come to give, then we leave. I have helped out many since I have been in this state, and I continue because I love this work. I have never been at my gravesite for very long. The grave is a repository for bones and ashes, but not spirit. We honor the dead by 'visiting' them at a grave . . . hogwash! I am more alive and more willing than I ever was in body. If you believe death to be a sentence with a full stop at the end, that's okay, but the pain is in the suffering of those left behind. If we can move on, however, the suffering will ease, and many more can learn that Spirit is always there to help."

༻ஐ༺

Sally's Dress
by Rod J. Ignacio

Last year, a lady named Sally, whom I worked with at the post office, passed away. She was like a mom to me and treated me like a son. I could always count on her in times of need.

I know that Sally is one of my angels. She would often visit me in my dreams. One dream occurred about a month after her passing. As I was talking to her in my dream, I noticed that she was wearing a dress with a floral print. I never saw her in this sort of dress when she was living.

The next day at work, a co-worker who was also close to Sally showed me a photograph sent to her by Sally's mother. That picture was of Sally wearing the same floral dress I had seen in my dream.

༻ஐ༺

Grandpa's Back
by Debra Pristo

My dear grandma passed away in November of 1997. I frequently woke up from dreams knowing that I'd had conversations with her as she sat by the side of my bed. I don't remember what was said, just her presence.

Then my grandfather passed in December of 1999. The following May, I had a dream, although it's as real today as it was a year and a half ago. I was in a room without walls, kind of grayish-white foggy walls, with my grandmother and others. I don't know who they were, but I know I knew them.

Like a phone in my head, I heard Grandpa say, in a voice he had 30 years ago, "Debra, I'm back and I'm fine." I was confused, and he repeated this two more times, adding that I should tell Grandma. I was filled with incredible excitement as I relayed this message to Grandma, and I woke up with the best feeling I had ever experienced.

However, I was confused. Why was I relaying a message to Grandma when I thought they were together? What did he mean by "I'm back"? Was he referring to being back on Earth, to being reincarnated? This experience was as real as my trip to the grocery store this morning, and it jump-started my own spiritual journey.

❦❦❦❦

"Everything Will Be Okay"
by Susan Huntz-Ramos

On February 1, 1995, my youngest daughter was born. My mother was unable to be with me because she was staying at the hospital with her older brother, who had fallen off a ladder the week before. At the time, I didn't know how serious his accident was. They didn't want to worry me during my pregnancy.

When my daughter was about five days old, my deceased grandfather came to visit me in my dreams. He walked tall, something my grandfather hadn't been able to do during the last 40 years of his life. He held my hand and walked with my two other children and me. He told me that he couldn't stay long, as he had to go see my sister, Kip, and my cousin, Patrice. Both of them were seriously ill.

Grandpa had a message that he needed to get across to me. He just wanted me to know that "everything will be okay." He kept saying that over and over. He told me to give that message to my family, too.

When I woke up, I was bothered by the dream. I never knew my grandfather when he was able to stand tall. I thought, *Oh, it was just a dream.* But still, it bothered me, so I called my dad. This is a man who doesn't believe in those kinds of things. Well, when I told him my story, my dad just got silent and said to me, "Sue, I think you had a very special visitor last night." I got the chills, and I knew then that it had to be real if my dad felt it, too.

Over the next few days, both my father's sister-in-law and my mom's brother passed away. But thanks to Grandpa's message, our family was comforted. It's a wonderful feeling when the angels and spirits are around, and I hope that when I pass into the afterlife, I will have the opportunity to come back and help someone else like I have been helped.

❧❧❧

"Eat Fish"
by Lynn Geosits

In 1987, my favorite uncle, Lou Garrett, passed away. About six months later, Uncle Lou appeared to me in the dream state. He stood next to a woman who was dressed as a nurse. "Eat fish!" he told me. Then he disappeared.

I felt energized by his visit, yet I had so many things I wanted to talk to him about that I was disappointed he was gone and had only told me to eat fish! I had been a vegetarian for almost 20 years, and his message was difficult for me to hear. It took me a year to add fish to my diet, but eventually I did so. I was living on the West Coast at the time, and I came to enjoy the fresh fish. Then I moved inland and disregarded his message again.

Soon afterward, I developed a tremor in my nervous system and head. The neurologist said I would have it the rest of my life and that there was no cure. Frustrated with her dismal diagnosis, I contacted a medical intuitive. She said I was suffering from malnutrition and needed more protein. She said that I had overdone the soy and beans, and my body needed other sources of protein and iodine.

I immediately remembered the visit from my uncle and realized that he was guiding me about this even before I had gotten sick. I followed the intuitive's advice and added fish back into my diet. Now, the tremor is totally gone! If I had been more diligent in following my uncle's message, I probably wouldn't have gotten the condition in the first place. I know that Uncle Lou was my angel that day and saw what I needed! Incidentally, in real life he had been a chiropractor and had been very interested in new techniques of healing.

❦❦❦

Extra Time with Dad
by Tatia Manahan-Heine

In January of 2001, I got married for the first time. Eleven days later, my father was found dead. I was horrified to hear the news, since Dad seemed fine at the wedding. I later found out that when I had walked down the aisle, he turned to friends in the wedding audience and said, "My job is now done here." It was as if he knew he was going to die less than two weeks later.

As I traveled to my parents' home, I cried the whole way on the plane. I cried so hard that my body shook. Since my dad didn't talk much about religion or spirituality, I was unsure how and where he was in heaven. I asked God three specific questions: "Is Dad with You?" "What time did he die?"(the coroner determined that he died some time on Tuesday, but he wasn't discovered until Wednesday), and "Is he happy where he is?"

I received my answer in Dad's poignant way when I arrived at my parents' house. My dad worked for Columbia Gas in Ohio, and he knew a lot about heating systems, so I knew that Dad was making his presence known when the heat went out in the house. A repairman said that a heating switch had been turned off, yet nobody had been in the house, and it's unlikely that anyone but Dad would have known about this particular switch.

I wanted to feel close to Dad, so I took some blankets and told my mother that I was going to sleep in Dad's bed while she and my sister slept downstairs. But as soon as I said that, the lights blew out. I guess Dad didn't want me to sleep in his bed for some reason!

So, I went to sleep in another room, and Dad came to me in an extremely vivid dream. I just knew that it was him—*I saw him!* He was glowing. Dad told me that he was okay and not to worry anymore. He said that he was with my mom's side of the family. Her two deceased brothers greeted him, and he repeated that I shouldn't worry. And then, as if in answer to my question to God about what time Dad had died, I saw Dad walking. He looked at a clock and started to fall, and the clock said 8:42 P.M. Then, everything went to black, so I took this to mean that that was the time he made his transition to the other side.

During the dream visitation, I saw perfectly what Dad was wearing. The next day, I was able to tell the funeral director what my father was wearing before he handed us Dad's clothing and belongings. And I wasn't surprised that what the funeral director handed me was the exact clothing I had seen Dad wearing in my dream visitation.

Dad must have been visiting the whole family and neighbors, too, because nobody knew of my dreams yet, and they started mentioning that they saw Dad that previous night in their dreams. At first, my mom—who didn't see Dad in a dream—didn't believe me, until I asked her about her two brothers whom I saw with Dad in the afterlife plane. There was no other way that I could have known that information.

I feel so blessed to have the opportunity to spend a little extra time with my dad. When I miss him, I ask for a sign, and within minutes, Dad's favorite song plays on the radio to let me know he's with me.

❦❦❦❦

A Comforting Earth Angel
by Anonymous

My dear nephew recently passed away at the age of 35 after a long struggle with malignant melanoma. He lived his last months with his parents in Chile, and the only thing that I, his godmother, could do for him from my home in the United Kingdom was pray for him. I began to pray every day to his angels to be with him and to give him faith, as well as comfort from his pain.

One night, I dreamed that I was there with my nephew at a family gathering. Everybody was wearing white clothes, and although it was a wedding celebration, everyone was looking sad and silent. I found him sitting on an armchair looking very weak and thin. He was surrounded by a group of good friends in white robes who were very cheerful and happy to be with him and protect him. I woke up feeling sure that I had seen his angels in my dream.

The morning after my nephew passed away, I went into a church to pray for him. As I left, a young man came walking down the street who looked exactly like my nephew! Even his way of walking and the type of clothes looked like his. I had to stop and stare in amazement, so the lad smiled . . . and his smile was also like my dear nephew's. Of course it was no apparition— he was a real person—but the "coincidence" was very striking.

❧❧❧

The End of the Nightmares
by Charlton Archard

It was August 1978, just before school was about to start. My three brothers, two sisters, and I had all received new bicycles that summer. We'd all ridden our bikes to our annual dentist appointment. My sister, Elizabeth, was first to be in and out of the dreaded chair. She rode up the street to my step-father's law firm to see him, but he was busy with a client, so Elizabeth decided to head home alone. That was the last time we would see her alive.

She was accosted one mile from home, driven to a dump in the woods, raped, and murdered. The man responsible for her death was tracked down, tried, and sentenced to18 years to life in prison. Needless to say, my family struggled with the devastation of this crisis. I was 12 at the time, and the youngest in the family.

I began having recurring nightmares, but one night, Elizabeth visited me in my dreams. At first, my dream that night started out like so many others: I was alone at home, it was dark, and I was terrified. I was sitting on my bed when I heard footsteps in the house. I immediately went to the closet, got in, and closed the door. I could hear the footsteps growing louder and closer. I could see this person coming to kill me. The person entered my room and walked right up to the closet door. After what seemed like an eternity, the door slid slowly open. Elizabeth stood in front of me, hands held out. She said, "It's okay, Charlton, you can come out now."

The nightmares ended after that. I have kept my sister, Elizabeth, close to me all these years, and I've just named my baby girl after her.

❀❀❀

Pop-Pop, My Miracle Angel
by Jessica Grzybowski

As a young girl struggling in the sixth grade, I was a very disorganized student. I would come to school and think, *Oh no! I have a test today, and I didn't even study for it!* I continued this behavior every week, unable to get it together. The teachers knew that I had the ability to excel in school, and they had me take part in enrichment programs, but I just couldn't apply myself.

One early morning, I awoke to the ringing of the telephone. I just knew something had happened to my grandfather, whom I called "Pop-Pop." Somehow, I knew he had died. And, indeed, he had.

My family immediately headed to my grandmother's house in Long Island, New York, for the wake and burial. The emotions of grief were so strong among our large family. But there was one specific moment that I remember the most.

My two younger brothers were talking with my grandmother in her bedroom. She was giving them some of Pop-Pop's World War II memorabilia as a gift to help them remember his presence. I was really upset because I wished I had something to keep close to my heart as well, but I didn't receive anything.

Because of the funeral, I missed over a week of school, and it was extremely difficult to catch up. As I sat in my bedroom trying so hard to complete all my missed assignments, I started crying uncontrollably. I felt like I was pinned under something heavy, and I had no concept of how to get out. My emotional outburst lasted for probably two hours until I just couldn't cry any longer. I felt so lost!

That night, I went to sleep, and I had the most amazing dream. I was at my grandmother's house with all my relatives. We were sitting in the dining room having a big dinner, as we had done so many other times before. My grandfather sat at the head of the table, and he ate his favorite food: mashed potatoes. I remember looking up at him, and then he spoke to me. He said, "I'm sorry, honey, that I don't have anything for you." I just looked up at him, and I felt like everything was okay.

After that experience, my life turned around in so many ways. Academically, I was a completely different person. It was as if the old version of me didn't even exist. I was awarded "Most Improved Student" for the year. The following two years, I became valedictorian of my seventh- and eighth-grade classes. I graduated from high school 10th in my class, out of 460 students.

I attribute my gifts to my Pop-Pop. His visitation was a true gift. I still have dreams of him to this day. I can feel his presence when I visit my relatives in New York. He was my angel, my guiding spirit who cleared all the fear out of my heart. Without that fear, I was able to accomplish miracles!

❦❦❦

A Clear and Comforting Dream Visit
by Lyn

My mother, Kathleen, was a wonderful, extremely gener-
ous woman who suffered a great deal in the last years of her
life. She finally died of cancer, and I was very distressed about
her death and what she had been through.

About two nights after her funeral, I had a dream in which I
heard the phone ring. I answered it, and it was my mother. I spoke
to her exactly as I would have in life. Her voice was clear, and
her manner of speaking was just like how she used to speak.

My mother asked how I was, and I quickly replied and
asked how she was. She said she was good. I asked if it was
better where she was now. With considerable emphasis, she
said, "Oh, yes, it's much better." I began to say that I was
sorry I hadn't done as much as I would have liked to for her.
She said, "Oh, that's all right," and then as I tried to talk more
to her, the connection just faded out.

Fifteen months after having this dream, it is as clear to me
now as it was then. The dream comforted me quite a bit.

❦❦❦

Love Poured All Over Me
by Tracy Cockerton

I had a dream about being at a festival or ceremony in
Burma. My mother-in-law's grandmother was there. She was
a small, dark, elegant Burmese lady in ceremonial dress. I had
been watching the festivities, when she came up to me and gave
me a Buddhist blessing.

There was someone, a Western woman, sitting farther
down from me asking no one in particular what they were

doing, in an ignorant kind of way. Grandmother Nat-thamé (a high Buddhist rank she attained) took my face in her hands and said to me, "Don't try to explain it to them; they won't understand." She poured so much love on me that I didn't want her to go when the dream ended soon after. I said, "I love you, don't go!"

I woke up in the morning, still with the overwhelming feeling of love that had been showered over me. Subsequently, I spoke to my mother-in-law, and she confirmed the description of her grandmother, whom I had never met in life. She also told me that she had been praying to her, asking her to look after me.

The meaning of Grandmother's message was clear. I have been learning reiki, feng shui, and pranic healing in the last few years, something my parents don't understand. I had been trying to explain the importance of these new interests to them, telling them that they were not just hocus-pocus, airy-fairy pursuits, but I could not. "Don't try," Grandmother had said. To date, I have not said a thing, and my parents haven't asked. Maybe one day they will understand.

꙰ ꙰ ꙰

CHAPTER FIVE

Mysterious Strangers

Alec's Guardian Angel
by Diane Bridges

When my son, Alec, was two years old, we were having some work done at our house. The workers asked if I would go down the hill to Duke's (which was an old-fashioned hamburger stand) to get them burgers. I took my husband's new car, which I was not used to driving. It had a console shift between the seats. Alec came with me. When we got to Duke's, I left Alec in his car seat, locked the door, and went up about ten feet to the window to order the hamburgers.

All of a sudden, I saw Alec reach over and move the gear shift out of "Park." The car started rolling backwards since Duke's was on an incline. I ran to the car to try to unlock it, but I couldn't stop it from rolling. All those stories you hear about mothers picking up boulders and trees resulting from a rush of adrenaline just didn't happen to me. I absolutely could not stop the car, and now it was out on Pacific Coast Highway.

I was hysterical, but still running alongside the car, trying to unlock it. All of a sudden, the car stopped with a jolt. I looked up, and there was a man holding the car from behind. He told me to unlock the car, get in, and start the car. I did what he said, pulled back into the parking lot, and immediately stopped the car to get out and thank him, but he was gone. I never saw where he came from or where he went!

❦❦❦

A Burden Is Lifted
by Jamie Gullo

My mother was a bus driver who transported handicapped preschoolers. She wasn't happy with her job, though, for various reasons. One day she was depressed and crying, and this little old man came to her bus door and told her that everything was going to be okay. He also told her that she was very beautiful. Then he left.

She didn't know where he went, but she felt better, like a big weight had been lifted off her shoulders. The rest of the day, she was in a good mood. She has never seen this man at her school before, and she never saw him again.

But his prophecy of things getting better came true! On the following Friday, my mother was offered a better job working at a day-care center. Her new boss even offered to help my mother open her own day-care center, which is something she had always wanted to do. I believe that my mother was visited by her guardian angel. My mother loves her new job and will never forget this experience.

❦❦❦

Heavenly Strength
by Kay H.

I was on my way from Arizona to Idaho with two huge Ryder truckloads of property. I had just had a baby by C-section six weeks prior. Joey, a girlfriend, offered to help me drive one of the trucks. We opened the back door of one truck in Nevada, and a water softener fell out of the door onto the ground. It had taken two big, strong men to put that water softener in the truck the day before, and they had been huffing and puffing. Apparently, the filter system was full of water, and they couldn't get it entirely drained.

There was little chance that my girlfriend and I could pick it back up four feet from the ground and put it back in the truck. We tried, but we couldn't even budge it.

So I said, "Joey, let's pray. The Lord says He wants us to ask to receive, so let's pray." She said, "You're right." So we prayed, walked around to secure the rest of the truck, and returned to the back of the Ryder truck.

Out of the corner of my eye, I saw a young man coming out from behind a dumpster, about 30 feet away. At first, his sudden appearance startled me, and I thought, *What if he's a weirdo?* and *Why was he hiding back there?* But a sudden peace came over me, and something told me not to be afraid of him.

The man walked with his head down, with an attitude of determination. He was under six feet tall, and built about average, with normal-size arms, not particularly well muscled. He was light-haired, with pleasant, soft features. He carried a tote bag that seemed to be light, as if it was stuffed with newspapers. I was surprised to see that he was in a short-sleeved shirt with no jacket. It was very cool that morning.

He walked right over to Joey and me and asked, "Do you need some help?" I thought, *There is no way that this small guy can put that water softener in the truck, what with two big guys struggling yesterday.*

Skeptically I said, "Well, this fell out, and we're trying to put it back."

He asked, "Do you want it back in there?" He seemed to be asking permission to put the water softener in the truck. I thought, *Well, duh, that's what I just said, but you aren't going to be able to do it. You're not big enough.* And I said aloud, "Yes," as I glanced around for another man—or, better yet, two men—who might be nearby who might help him lift it in the back of the truck again. But there was no one else around.

Wordlessly, he leaned over the water softener, picked it up without a single grunt, as if he was picking up a large tubular pillow, and he set it in the truck effortlessly, without even climbing up the back with it in his arms—totally by himself! Joey and I both stood there with our mouths agape. I managed to say, "Thank you."

I thought, *I should offer this guy some money*, as I always do when someone helps me. I turned around, but he was gone. I walked all the way around the truck quickly to see if I could spot him to offer him something, as no one could walk that fast. The only thing that could have hidden him was the dumpster, since he had walked in the direction of a huge parking area as huge as a ten-acre field with few cars in it. But he had totally disappeared as if he had vanished into thin air!

I thought, *Well, maybe we didn't have the water softener in the right position, or maybe it was caught on something or stuck in a pothole.* To experiment, I climbed in the truck and tried to move the water softener just an inch or two. After all, if the average-sized man lifted it so effortlessly, surely I could move it a little bit. But I couldn't even drag it an inch or twist it into another position! It was like a solid block of concrete that was cemented onto the truck's bed. Even Joey and I together couldn't get it to budge an inch.

Joey and I looked at each other, and she said, "Let's get out of here." It took us both a while to accept what we had seen, and we mentioned it several times during the trip, remarking how faithful God was to His children. I have marveled at this experience for five years, and to this day, I still say, "Wow!"

❦❦❦

The Camp Angel
by Daniel R. Person

I was at Covenant Pines Christian Camp in McGregor, Minnesota, at family camp with my parents, brother, and sister. Every morning we had a mandatory church service. I was about seven years old and more interested in playing than going to church. So I told my mother I was sick and couldn't go. When they left, I went down to the lake and went swimming.

I was a poor swimmer and not allowed in the deep end. I thought that this was my chance, and I crossed under the *H*-shaped dock into the deep end. After being there for a minute, I swallowed some water and began to thrash. I struggled for a little while and went underwater. I looked up and saw the light through the water. I quit struggling and put my hand up out of the water as I went still and began to sink.

Just as my hand was about to go under, I shot up onto the dock. I was on my knees, throwing up at a man's feet. I looked up, and he asked if I was okay. I said yes, and he turned and walked away. I crawled off of the dock and stayed on the beach for a little while. Then I walked back to my cabin when I felt better.

I slept the rest of that day and looked for the man at dinner that night. There were only about 70 people there, and I spent the rest of the weekend looking for him. He wasn't there. The camp was in the middle of nowhere, so he wouldn't have been there if not for the camp (or to save my life!).

❀❀❀

William White
by Dawn Elizabeth Allmandinger

In the 1980s, I was married to a man who physically abused me. We both worked at the same restaurant. I was a waitress, and he was a busboy. He would say mean things to me in front of my co-workers, and once I came into work with a black eye, covered with heavy makeup.

One day, a man and woman whom I had never seen before came into the restaurant. The man started to ask me things about myself, and then he said that I was special. But I didn't think that was true at the time because my ex-husband had always told me otherwise, as had my father.

He asked me what I thought my mission in life was. Without thinking, I said, "Well, I'm God's helper." The man told me that not many people know that about themselves. He asked me how I thought I helped people. I told him that I hug people, and I can feel what's going on inside of them.

He told me that I was right about how I felt, and that I should give the woman who was with him (his sister) a hug and tell them what I felt. I did give her a hug, and I told her I felt she was not happy and that she was going through some kind of move that she was uneasy about. The woman confirmed that she *was* going through a move, that she wasn't sure if it was the right thing to do, and she wasn't real happy about it. I couldn't believe that I had gotten it right!

William told me that he felt I was a healer, which I had been told twice before, but I didn't think I was special enough to be a helper of God. Now, these two people didn't know me from Adam, and the man seemed to know things about me and my life that no one did. He told me that I wouldn't be with my husband much longer, which at that time, I didn't believe. I really thought of marriage as a "death do us part" commitment.

The man then asked me if I wanted his phone number, and I said yes. Now what's strange about this, is that the restaurant where I worked was really busy at the time of his visit, with the lunch rush. Yet, the only people seated at my station were the man and his sister. That gave me time to talk with them.

So, I opened my address book to a blank page, and he wrote, "William White, 758-6055." Then he said, "Look at my name. See, it says, 'Will I Am' in it!" William asked me to call him so that I could join a group of helpers and healers.

A few days later, I called the number, and all I heard was a recording that said the number had been changed and that there was no new number.

I did end up divorcing my husband, as William predicted. I am now ready to forgive my dad for the abuse, as well as my ex-husband.

I have looked for William White ever since then, with no luck. I truly believe that he was an angel in human form trying to guide me back on the path to peace.

❦❦❦

An Angel to the Rescue
by David Guiron

I saw an angel six years ago in Jacksonville, Florida, while I was working as a repairman for a water softening company. It was about 4 or 5 P.M., and I was lost in a secluded area, trying to find my next customer's address.

I pulled off the road and got stuck in the mud and soft grass. I prayed for some help. After about 20 minutes, an older gentleman in a truck pulled over and offered to help me. He assisted in pulling my truck out of the mud and grass, and I thanked him. He then drove back the way he came. I proceeded to drive behind him because I had to find an area to turn around. I then saw his truck speed up and disappear into thin air. I know that was an angel who came to help me.

꒐꒐ ꒐꒐ ꒐꒐

CHAPTER SIX

Angel Signs, Lights, and Clouds

An Angel Who Descended from the Clouds
Susan Moore

My grandmother was in the hospital for major heart surgery, with a 50-50 chance of survival. After surgery, she never
woke up from the anesthesia, and she was in a coma for two
weeks. I lived about 90 minutes away from the hospital, and I
visited her every other day with my mother. One particular day,
though, I didn't want to make the long drive to the hospital, so
I stayed home. I was horrified when Grandma passed away at
5 A.M. the next day. This really bothered me, because I didn't
get to see her one more time.

That evening, I went into the kitchen in the dark, looking
out the back door. I said aloud, "Why did you leave me? I didn't
get to say good-bye or even give you one last kiss!" I started
to cry again—then something caught my attention.

I saw this funnel-shaped cloud come down from the sky.
It almost looked like a tornado was coming my way. Then this
funnel cloud started to take shape, and I stood mesmerized. This
cloud started to turn into a beautiful woman! She had long white
hair and a long white dress on, with some sort of rope tied
around her waist.

Then she started to reach out with her arms and float toward me. She was suspended about five feet off the ground, and she was about six feet tall. When she lifted her arms, her long sleeves were hanging and flapping in the wind. When she got about three feet in front of me, I ran! I was petrified, so I ran to get my husband to come see this. I knew that no one would believe me, so I wanted him to witness this amazing sight.

When I finally got him, though, she was gone, and the only thing left was a thick fog sitting about two feet above the ground. Then we looked at our neighbors' homes, and we were the only one with fog in the backyard. I truly believe that this was an angel coming to let me know that my grandmother was okay and in a better place. I often wonder what would have happened if I had stayed to see the angel instead of running. It has been five years since this happened, and I can still see the vision in my mind like it happened yesterday.

๛๛๛

Flashes of Angel Lights
by Gretchen Mahon

I had just finished reading Doreen's book *Angel Visions*. I tried following some of the steps to see my own angels, with no success. I admit I had my doubts, and this was probably the reason I had no luck.

A short time later, I was talking with my seven-year-old son, Thomas, about his recent miraculous recovery from an illness. I told Thomas that he must have had a guardian angel looking after him to make him well. I proceeded to tell him that I thought his guardian angel was his deceased Grandfather Thomas, whom he was named after. Grandpa Tom died seven years before he was born, but Thomas's father often told him how Grandpa Tom was looking down from heaven on all of us.

Thomas suddenly stared off into space and said he saw a light flash in one corner and then the other. I saw nothing. He then proceeded to stare off into space, mesmerized. He said he saw another flash of light, this one like a big hand reaching into the air. Again, I saw nothing. He did this a third time and said he saw the light again.

By this time, I had goose bumps and could feel my heart pounding. I had never discussed anything I had read in Doreen's book with Thomas, so he would not know that angels sometimes appear as a flash of light. I wouldn't have known this either without having read the book only a short time ago. I'm convinced that those flashes of light my young son saw were signs of his guardian angel, his Grandpa Tom. I don't know how I know this. I just felt it when he told me he saw the lights. It was as if my deceased father-in-law was saying, "Yes, I am your guardian angel, and I want you to know I'm here." I will never forget this experience as long as I live.

ﷺﷺﷺ

Safe and Sound
by Suzanne Chaney

My husband and I were driving in a small rental car from Kentucky to New York City. The first part of the trip was very nice and quite scenic. But as we started nearing the peaks of the Appalachians, the skies grew continually more ominous. Soon we were driving in heavy snow, on slick roads. We slowed our pace to a crawl, but large semi-trucks kept blowing past us, and the wind they created pushed us all over the road. The sides of the roads were marked with

No Stopping signs, so we continued as best we could. We were incredibly scared.

At that time, I said a prayer for God to send angels to help us on our journey, to bless those driving with good judgment, and to protect us from danger. Immediately after raising my head from the prayer, I looked out my window at the storm clouds.

In the midst of the dark, ominous sky was one bright, white cloud in the shape of an angel's face. It also had glowing, luminescent wings. The sun peeked above the edges of this cloud, causing it to shine brightly with beams of bright light shooting from its edges. My eyes swelled with tears, and I knew that my prayer had been answered.

We spent two more hours traveling on the snow-slicked roads, but it was a whole different experience. The semi-trucks' wind no longer seemed to affect our car. Throughout the two-hour period, I continued to glimpse angels in the clouds, but nothing as brilliant as the first sighting.

The clouds seemed to be a sign from the angels, saying, "We're still here with you." The fear left my heart. We arrived safely in New York City several hours later, and despite the grueling drive, I felt invigorated and light, like everything in the world was right. What a glorious gift we received!

❦❦❦

The Guiding Light
by Dorene Graham

I've always believed in angels. I know they've been a part of my life from the start, so it wasn't unusual for me to call on them to help me that dark morning after hurricane Opal blew through Atlanta as a tropical storm. Opal tore the ridge pole off our roof and knocked the power out for three days in our complex.

We lost power sometime in the night, and Jessie, my eight-year-old daughter, found her way down to my basement room and woke me in the darkness before dawn. She was frightened. I tried to comfort her and wanted to invite her to crawl into the bed, but it was only a double, and I already had her two sisters snuggled in with me. There wasn't any room, so I encouraged her to go back to bed. Guilt weighed heavy on my heart as she felt her way back up the stairs.

I wanted to immediately go after her, but I couldn't get my body to move. I was extremely tired, although conscious nonetheless. Agitated that I couldn't go to her, I said a quick prayer, asking the angels to watch over her and not let her be afraid.

Within minutes, a light shone down on the stairwell. It grew bigger, and it was glowing. Relief flowed through me. I figured that my husband was awake and had lit the oil lamp and was heading down the stairs. I called to him, wanting to direct him to Jessie. The light glowed brighter, then seemed to stop moving. It glowed down that stairwell for just a moment or two, but then it faded and went out.

I was left in the dark again, with the realization that the oil lamp wouldn't have disappeared like that; it would have moved away. Also, the house was extremely quiet—no rustled movements, no creaking stairs broke that stillness. The suspicion crept into my mind that it hadn't been my husband with the lamp, and I realized that an angel had answered my prayer.

The next morning, I asked Jessie about the light. Her eyes widened, and she nodded, saying that she had seen the angel, although she felt somehow dazed at the time and could only stare. I believe she was awestruck, and her mind wasn't quite sure how to interpret it. It was almost as if I were helping her recall a dream. Sadly, when I asked her about it later, she couldn't remember it.

When my husband woke up, I questioned him, and he assured me that he hadn't been up earlier. Our electricity wasn't restored until three days later. What else could that light have been? I know in my heart that I saw the light of an angel.

❦❦❦

"Thank You, Raphael!"
by Sue Barrie

I am a 47-year-old mother of three boys, and I've just made it through the worst three years of my life! I truly believe that I've been guided, carried, comforted, and healed by the angels that surround me.

Three years ago, my husband and I divorced, then I moved, and my two oldest sons moved out. Throughout these stressful times, I turned more and more to spiritual help. I had always believed in the fact that we all have guardian angels. On two occasions when I felt I couldn't take any more, I felt a hand ever so gently stroke my cheek, and once I felt someone patting me on the head very softly.

A few months later, I discovered a lump in my breast. I instinctively knew that it was cancer, but for some reason I felt calm and had the knowledge that I would beat it. I prayed to my angels each night for healing and strength, and each day, I woke up with an inner confidence.

My surgery went well, and after having a mastectomy, I came home two days after surgery. I barely took a painkiller as I prayed regularly to the Archangel Raphael, and I was visited and comforted on two occasions.

The first night, I woke up with some discomfort, feeling a little lonely and sorry for myself. But then as I stirred, I felt the sensation of arms wrapped around the upper parts of my legs, as though someone was holding me close to comfort me. I went back to sleep instantly.

The following night, I was having difficulty finding a comfortable position to sleep. I had just completed my prayer for healing when I detected the distinct smell of coconut oil! Then I heard a sort of shuffle in my room in a corner to the right of me.

I turned onto my back, and as I did so, I got a tremendous shock. High above me on my ceiling were dozens of tiny twinkling lights, almost like miniature glowworms. They wiggled and shone only in the area directly above me! I was awestruck and elated, as I knew at that moment that I had been visited by my angels, and the healing was beginning both spiritually and physically for me!

I feel so full of love and joy these days, and I see beauty in everything. This has made me so excited that I tell everyone I can about this tremendous power and love! My biopsies show that there is no more cancer, and I'm overjoyed.

❦❦❦

Healing Angel Lights
by Nancy C. Badger

Last year, following an epidermal nerve block performed on his back, my husband, Kelly, became extremely sick. We called to report his symptoms for four days and were put off by the doctor each time, who stated that my husband probably had "the flu." Well, to make a long story short, my husband is now paralyzed and cannot walk. He cannot urinate or move his bowels without help. Staphylococcus aureus was introduced to his spine through the epidermal, creating spinal abscesses and meningitis.

I have prayed and asked God and the angels to watch over our family: *Help us to find the love in our hearts, the strength and courage we need as a family to endure this very challenging time in our lives.*

The other evening, I saw a confirmation of these prayers. I was awakened around three o'clock in the morning. Beside our bed was an image of a person. Floating across our room were dozens of little white flickers of light, as clear and bright as the lights on a Christmas tree. I lay very still watching these beautiful lights, while spasms shot through my husband's pelvis. I knew that the angels had come to help us. I find comfort in the fact that God and His angels are listening to our prayers.

❦❦❦❦

A Sign from Uncle Frank
by Angie Chiste

My Uncle Frank died in 1984, and my son was born in 1991. My son has had a long-time fascination with my deceased uncle. When he was about four years old, he would tell me how Uncle Frank would come to him at the playground at his day-care center and push him on the swing or talk to him.

I decided to give my son a little test. He had never seen a picture of my Uncle Frank. I showed him pictures of all my other uncles first. Then I showed him a picture of Uncle Frank, and my son knew exactly who he was! I thought he must have a special bond with him of some sort.

When my son entered first grade in 1996, we would drive past the cemetery on our way to and from school each day.

He would ask me questions about Uncle Frank, and then one day he told me that he wanted to visit his grave. I asked my mother where he was buried, and she could only give me the name of the corner in the cemetery.

One day, I picked up my son from school and we headed to the cemetery. We walked up and down the headstones, looking for my uncle. It was a cool fall day and very calm. After about 45 minutes of searching, my son started to whine; he was getting hungry. I was losing my patience. We were both getting tired and cranky. I finally looked up to the sky and said, "Sorry, Uncle Frank, I just can't find you today. We'll come back another day."

Just then, a huge gust of wind stirred the leaves behind me, which caused me to turn around. The moment I turned, the wind stopped. I looked down, and there was my Uncle Frank's grave. Right at my feet!

❦❦❦

A Call from My Angel
by Suzanne Goodnough

My husband and I attended Doreen's seminar at the Whole Life Expo in Chicago in October of 1999. At one point during the seminar, Doreen took everyone in the audience through a meditation, where we asked the guardian angel on our left to say his/her name to us. Then we proceeded with the guardian angel on the right. Doreen told us not to judge what we heard and not to let our ego get in the way.

Doreen told us that if we didn't believe what we heard, we were to ask for a sign of validation from the particular angel and wait to see what would happen. After the seminar, I asked my husband if he had gotten any names. He said, "Yes, the names Michael and Philip. Did you hear any names?"

"Yes," I replied. "The angel on the right said her name was Grace." I loved it—it was so spiritual and angelic of a name that I never questioned it. But the angel on the left said his name was Maurice. In my mind, I said, *Maurice! What a stupid name for an angel!* It made me think of Maurice Gibb of the Bee Gees, and I imagined a *Saturday Night Fever* disco angel, with a strobe light, white suit, and the works. I thought, *This can't be! I don't want a disco angel!*

That night during my evening prayers and meditation, I asked the angels for a sign. I said, "Please give me a sign that I just didn't make up the name Maurice." The next morning at eight o'clock, the telephone rang. We were still sleepy, so I didn't answer the phone, and the answering machine picked up the message.

When I retrieved the message, a male voice said, "I am looking to speak with Suzanne Goodnough. My name is Maurice. If you call this number and ask for this extension, I will be able to help you with your problem and get it all cleared up in two minutes. Looking forward to hearing from you." I saved the message so that my husband could listen to it.

I said to my husband, "Out of all the male names, can you believe this man's name is Maurice?" I returned the call shortly after and asked for the extension number the man had given in the message. A woman answered the phone. I told her who I was and asked to speak to Maurice.

She said, "My dear, I don't know who you talked to, but there is no one by the name of Maurice who works here." After that, I believed that my angel's name is Maurice.

(**Note from Doreen:** I was editing this while on a European Eurostar train, and twice, after this story was complete, I looked up to see the name Maurice on two different building signs!)

❦❦❦

Healing Angel
by Lily Alexandrovitch

On February 21, 1996, my cousin Cindy; her husband, Michael; my brother; and I went to the Ethel M chocolate factory in Las Vegas, Nevada. It had been raining all day and was still drizzling when we went into the factory. After purchasing chocolates, the three of them wanted to tour the grounds while I went to sit in the car, since it was chilly outside. All the other cars and tour buses had left. Although the sky above was still thick with dark clouds, it had stopped raining. Sitting in the back seat of the car, I looked out the side window on my right and noticed a beautiful, majestic mountain range that extended from behind the building on the left to behind the chocolate factory on the right.

I thought how unusual it was that the mountains were dark gray and purplish. The sky above them was light blue, although above the car, the sky was still hidden behind dark clouds. It looked as though the sun had just set behind the mountains, and the entire mountain ridge had a white glow above it. I couldn't help thinking how unusual it was, and that I had never seen anything like it. If anyone had painted an exact picture of the scene, everyone would say it was all wrong. I must have stared at this beautiful mountain for at least 20 minutes. Then my friends returned to the car.

I never said anything; I just continued looking at the mountains, since I was so mesmerized by them. No one said a word; we all just sat there and stared at them. Then Michael said, "If anyone painted a picture of the mountains looking like that, they would be told they had it all wrong, as it's too bright to be real"—my exact thoughts! We were all quiet and just kept looking. Around the middle of our view, the mountain range dipped down and then upwards, forming a large *V.* The sky behind the *V* was now also pale blue. Although I had never taken my eyes away, I now saw two glowing rays that looked like gigantic spotlights coming from behind the *V* in the mountain, up toward the sky.

Then right in the middle of these two rays, a white speck appeared. The speck quickly got bigger, and it now looked like a cloud, except that it was exceptionally bright. The cloud then started to take shape, first like a person, and then with wings on either side of it. It was an angel—a huge angel with large wings! The angel was turned slightly to the right. I suddenly thought that maybe I was the only one seeing this incredible sight, and without taking my eyes off it, I said, "I see an angel."

"It sure looks like an angel," said Michael. We sat in awe, just staring.

Remembering that Cindy had never had any religious training, I asked what she saw. Nervously laughing, she said, "I see an angel."

A few seconds later, the angel quickly shrank into a dot and then vanished into the pale blue sky from where it had originated. What a memorable experience!

)€)€)€

CHAPTER SEVEN

Visions of Jesus

Never Alone
by Kimberly McCright

When I was in college, I moved in with my grandparents since they lived in the same town as the university I was attending. After several months, I still had not made any friends or had any dates. I was very lonely. All around me every day, there were couples and groups of friends.

I grew very depressed, and one day while I was in the shower, I just broke down and cried. I became angry with God, wondering where He was, since I felt so cold and alone. I prayed to Jesus, and I begged him to come into my life and help me through this difficult time.

As I pulled back the curtain to step out of the shower, I saw an amazing sight. The mirror was completely fogged up, except for an outline of a face with long hair, a beard, and a mustache. I could also see the outline of eyes and a nose. It looked just like Jesus!

I couldn't believe my eyes and just stood there staring at it. I felt a wave of warmth and love and knew that I was never alone. I can't describe the healing that took place at that moment. I felt so special that Jesus would show himself to me in this way, to let me know that he is always here, always listening.

The fact that this happened to me, a "nobody," really made me feel special. I realized that each of us is equally important in God's eyes; we're all deserving of His love, and He never leaves us. Since then, I have never felt lonely. Very soon after that incident, I met my best friend, who introduced me to my husband.

❦❦❦❦

"Is Jesus Over Your House?"
by Sherry L. Gunderson

I had recently read Doreen's book *Angel Visions*, and I started praying that I could have a vision of my own. Nothing happened immediately, but about a week later, I had a dream that really didn't make sense to me at the time.

In my dream, I was awakened from my sleep by a phone call from my friend Ernie.

"Hello," I said to him.

"Sherry," he asked, "is Jesus over your house?" He said it with such amazement in his voice.

I was lying on my back with the phone to my ear, looking at the ceiling from left to right and shaking my head as I answered, "No, I don't see Jesus." This dream didn't make any sense to me. In fact, I took it to mean that I wasn't religious enough.

A week later as I drove home from work, a colorful glitter in the sky caught my eye. I glanced to my left and saw what looked like the face of Jesus surrounded by a yellow light. I remember peeking over my sunglasses, asking myself if the other drivers around me could see what I was seeing.

Before I knew it, it was time for me to turn right and head north, as I was just a few minutes from my house. I was surprised that a vision of Jesus was still in the clouds. The only difference now was that he was looking up instead of straight ahead. I also noticed that he was wearing what looked like a bandana (I have been told it is the crown of thorns). I couldn't believe what I was seeing.

My sister's friend Pete was outside near my car. I pointed to the sky and asked him, "Tell me if that is Jesus, or am I seeing things?"

Pete looked up to the vision and said, "*That* is Jesus."

I didn't relate the two happenings until I realized that in my dream, when my friend Ernie asked, "Sherry, is Jesus over your house?" it was supposed to prepare me for what I was about to see a week later.

❧❧❧

In the Arms of Love
by Gazelle

In October of 1999, I was going through an extremely difficult time. The details would take up a lot of space, but suffice it to say, I honestly didn't know if I would survive it. It was too much for me to cope with. I remember praying, pleading for help. I just couldn't take one more step on my own.

One night I woke up at about 4:45 A.M. and was totally awake. I'm one of those people who can take up to an hour to feel really alert, so this was very unusual for me. I walked out to the living room and sat for a few minutes, then I went back to bed thinking how very strange it all was. When I lay down in bed and relaxed again, there were images that came so strong to me that I thought I must be dreaming, but I had just gotten back in bed and knew I was awake.

The first image was of a magnificent angel who was absolutely beautiful! I knew it was a male form with short hair. His wings were huge and he was all in white . . . white wings, white robe, white hair. The next thing I noticed was that the room was full of angels—all sizes and shapes—some were just little flickers of light. Some had wings, but not all of them. The room seemed endless, yet it was full. There was so much peace and love. I kept saying, "I don't understand." It's like I was told telepathically that these were angels, but I had no idea why I was there.

The next thing I realized was that someone was holding me in their arms, as you would a baby. I tried to stand on my own, but my legs wouldn't hold me up, I wasn't strong enough, so he picked me up again and held me. I don't know who was holding me except that I knew it was a male. When I was up in his arms, I was facing the angels and trying to understand what was happening. Something or someone told me to look to the left. I can't begin to describe how profound the image was that I saw. It was sort of like an altar, but all I could see was the light. I know there were images behind the "altar," and I know one of them was Jesus. I remember thinking that one of them was God, but my conscious mind has difficulty accepting that.

I know I was given a choice of whether or not to accept something, but I'm still unsure as to exactly what I was being offered. All I know is that I said yes. At that point, I was sent a bolt of visible energy that was the color of sunshine. It went through my body like a thunderbolt. My body couldn't contain it all, and it went through me as it filled me and the whole room. I felt more peace, joy, healing, gratitude, and love than I will ever find words to describe. I had a feeling that everyone there was celebrating, that something very important had just happened, and they were rejoicing. The feeling of peace and well-being stayed with me, and I eventually drifted off to sleep.

The next day, I was thinking about it, and even though I still felt good, I began to think it was just a nice dream. I was standing at the stove cooking dinner when another bolt of the same energy went through my body. I could hardly stand up! I remembered hearing somewhere that you had to pass energy on, and this was too much energy for me to absorb, so I started sending it to all my family members and friends, but they couldn't absorb enough of it either, so I sent it to one hospital and then another and then another.

Finally, I started really focusing on the children's hospital. I placed a dome of healing white light over the building. I prayed that every single child would be given a reprieve that day, and every single parent would feel relief as they saw their child getting better. After a while, the energy slowed down, and I realized that I was still standing in my kitchen, holding on to the counter. It was the exact same energy that had gone through me the night before, and that was when I knew for sure that it hadn't been a dream.

I still don't fully understand what happened to me that night. I had a very distinct feeling that I had been given a wonderful gift and that I was to do something very special with it. I'm still not sure what that is, but I believe it has something to do with healing myself as well as others. So in the meantime, I continue to do everything I can to heal myself, while learning as much as I possibly can about angels and staying open to their guidance. They're a part of my everyday life now. I recognize the angels' influences and *know* they're there, and I also know that when the time is right, I will know all I need to.

What I do know for sure is that the angels are there for everyone whether or not we realize it. They hear what we say, and they intervene in more ways than we'll ever know. They bring us peace, joy, and love, and will always act for our higher good . . . even if we don't think so at the time. Many wonderful things have happened to me since I started talking to the angels. The most loving wish I could have for someone is that they come to know their angels.

❦❦❦

So Much Love!
by Marsha Zaler

I had an amazing dream that I will never forget: I was all alone in this white room, wondering where I was. Out of the corner of my eye, I saw a glorious white light. When I turned to look, I saw the Sacred Heart of Jesus with his index finger pointing to his heart. He was looking down at me so lovingly that I couldn't take my eyes off of him. He was so beautiful, and the light was so full of love.

I looked up, and from the sky, the words "Jesus and Mary love you" appeared. Then the phrase fell to the ground with the loudest bang I had ever heard in my entire life. The entire "dream" was so moving that I woke up sobbing.

❦❦❦

The Incredible Brightness!
by Susan

I was a 19-year-old newly single mother living with my parents after the baby's father abandoned us. I had only been to church about ten times in my entire life. I had never read the Bible or prayed much. Then I had this life-changing dream.

In the dream, I walked from my bedroom in my parents' house into the living room. There, sitting at the dining room table, was Jesus, along with some other men dressed in the same style of clothing. It must have been nighttime in my dream, because I felt like my parents were sleeping in their bedroom. Jesus had this intense glow around him, and I was terrified.

Feeling very afraid, I ran to my parents' bedroom, trying to wake them up. I was screaming, "Go away!" to Jesus and the other men. But my parents didn't wake up. It felt like I was having a nightmare. Then, for some reason, I stopped crying and went back into the living room.

Jesus got up from the table, and he walked over to me. I was no longer scared. When he got close to me, I got on my knees. I remember how *extremely bright* he was, like an aura. His face was peaceful and beautiful. His robe was the very brightest white, with a blue stripe on it. As I remember the dream, what stands out the most was that Jesus was so intensely bright!

Then, while I was on my knees looking at him, I starting saying, "I'm so sorry," over and over. He touched me with his left hand. I didn't hear him say any words with his lips, but I somehow heard Jesus say, "I forgive you." When I heard him say these words, I felt warm, peaceful, happy, and filled with love. I had feelings that cannot be felt on this earth. I remember how very, very strong this feeling was. I felt like part of the brightness of Jesus, of this immense love and warmth together. Then I woke up. I couldn't figure out why I'd had this dream, but I knew how special it was, since it felt so real.

After the dream, I got a Bible and began reading it nightly. When I got to the parts about Jesus, I felt really strong emotions, because I felt like he was my brother and close friend.

❦❦❦

An Emotional Healing with Jesus
by Louise Ratcliffe

When I was seven years old, I had a traumatic experience at the Catholic elementary school that I attended. Learning seemed difficult for me, and as a timid child, I avoided asking my teachers questions or asking for their help. During my first spelling test, I had such little faith in my spelling ability that I felt that my only option was to cheat to pass the test. So cheat I did, in a ridiculously obvious manner. Well, much to my surprise, I was discovered.

As punishment, I was taken into the school storeroom and beaten on the hands with a ruler. The nun who carried out this cruel and humiliating beating was my teacher, Sister Anthony. My memories of her, which are as clear as yesterday—as well as the shame, hurt, and humiliation—have stayed with me all these years. Some may consider this to be a small issue, but to me it was huge.

From that day on, I spent the rest of my school years looking out the window. I switched off totally to any kind of English teaching and resigned myself to the fact that I was dumb. For many years, I held a deep resentment for Sister Anthony. By blaming her for my English shortcomings, I blocked any healing of the situation. For a long time, I was able to get away with my bad English.

But then I had to study so that I could pass a six-hour exam that would allow me to work at a real estate agency. I found the study time extremely stressful, as I constantly fought with the voice in my head that told me I was dumb and hopeless. Finally, I went into a meditation and asked Jesus and the angels to help me overcome my lack of belief in myself.

During my meditation, I met with Jesus. I saw and felt him say that he wished to take me on a journey. Jesus took me by the hand, smiled at me, and led me back into that classroom on that fateful day in 1969.

There stood Sister Anthony in the class full of children. But instead of looking cross, this time she walked over to me smiling, and she crouched down, looking into my eyes. Her face had lost its hardness, as I remembered it, and I felt overwhelming love and forgiveness *for her* and *from her.* It was so real!

Sister Anthony said that she was sorry for having hurt me, and that she was no longer on the earth. She told me that she loved me and that she would help me overcome my spelling problems. Sister Anthony said that all I had to do to attain her assistance was to ask.

I passed my real estate exam and am now taking English lessons. My spelling has steadily improved. I also discovered that I am mildly dyslexic, but I know I can overcome it, thanks to Jesus introducing me to my new angel called Sister Anthony.

❧ ❧ ❧

CHAPTER EIGHT

Answered Prayers

A Heavenly Jump-Start
by Sharon

I had to go into town, but when I went out to my car, I discovered that someone had left the door open. The open door meant that the interior light was on too long, and my battery was completely dead.

We had a spare battery, but it didn't fit my car's terminals. My husband and I tried jump-starting the car with it, but we had no success. Then my husband brought his car around and we tried jump-starting it from his battery. Still no luck. He increased the revs on his car, and I tried again . . . but still nothing.

Just as he was going back to his car to turn it off, I remembered the angels. I thought, *Raphael heals!* Then, in my mind, I cried out, *Raphael, heal my car!*

The car burst into life! I made it all the way into town without a hitch. What makes this story even more delightful is that I had to get into town before the bookstore closed. You see, I had just found out that they had Doreen's book *Angel Therapy* back in stock.

Instant Assistance
by Joanne

My son, Rusty, was a bright and extremely happy child. He was full of energy and curiosity, and was very impulsive. One day I was busy in the kitchen, preparing a meal. Rusty was playing nearby. He was not yet two years old.

As I was cooking, I laid a steak knife on the countertop. I turned away for an instant, and Rusty grabbed the knife. When I turned back, he was smiling, ready to bolt with his prize, and expecting a gleeful chase. Still unstable as a toddler, it was a tragedy in the making. Nothing I could have said or done would have stopped that little boy from completing his purpose. I fell to my knees and pleaded with God's angels for help. No words came from my mouth. I simply flashed thoughts instantaneously. Rusty, still joyful and full of energy, dropped the knife. It happened so quickly and was so uncharacteristic of the chase games he initiated that I knew angels had been with us that day. I thanked the angels and God for helping me that day. I also became even more aware of all the good that surrounds my son!

❦❦❦

Whatever Help You Need
by Julie Annette Bennett

On Thursday night, November 18, 1999, I woke up to the drip, drip sound of the rain hitting the gutter. As I slowly emerged from a sound slumber, I just knew I wouldn't be able to get back to sleep if the bothersome noise continued.

I decided to call on the help of my angel guides: "Please, angels, I won't be able to get back to sleep unless the drip, drip sound stops. Please intercede for me and stop that racket." About 30 seconds rolled by with no relief, so I prayed again for their intervention and added, "Now, please."

Within ten seconds, the dripping sound stopped. Not slowly, not sporadically—it just stopped. Thank you, my lovely angels.

❦❦❦

The Parking Space Angel
by Brendan Glanville

I was driving through Brisbane City, here in Australia, and I was late to hear a friend make a political speech for the Queensland government. Then I remembered that we could ask angels to find us a parking space. Immediately upon asking, I heard a voice say, *Turn left, then left again.* This actually sent me in the wrong direction, but I decided to trust it and follow the directions.

Then I heard, *Turn around.* I did so immediately, into a driveway of a building. To my left, as if it was waiting for me, was a metered parking space. Then I realized that I'd forgotten my wallet in my haste, and I needed money for the parking meter. So I asked my angels for change, and when I opened my ashtray, I found the exact two coins that I needed for the meter. I was so excited upon walking in to my meeting that I called my office and told my staff.

Returning to my car after the speech, I said to the angels, "If any human needs a parking space, this one has time left on the meter, and that person can have it for free." I got in my car, and before I even started it, a car came around the corner and waited until I pulled out of my space.

❦❦❦

Protected from a Tornado
by Judy Mitchell

In the spring of 1996, we were on a "tornado watch" where I lived in Allison, Arkansas. It was a hot, humid Sunday, and the sky was a greenish gray. Having recently moved to Arkansas from California, I was unfamiliar with tornadoes. I had seen an unusual thing in the sky the day before: a complete circular rainbow around the sun. I found out later that it's called a Sundog, and it indicates severe weather.

I was home baby-sitting a friend's son. My 13-year-old foster daughter was with me, as well as my twins, who were 8, and they were all playing inside the historic old house we were renting. I received a phone call from a neighbor saying that there was a large tornado on the ground moving toward our home! She said we needed to take cover. Well, there was no basement, only a bathroom on an outside wall with a large window. I knew from what I had read that this was not sufficient protection.

I told all of the children to get their shoes on and get into the tub. The sky was growing darker and greener. I went outside to look, and there it was; I could hear it before I saw it. It was huge, spinning, and it was about a quarter mile from us. I ran back into the house to get to the children, and then everything went dark—all the electricity went off. The noise of the tornado approaching was so loud that it was almost unbearable. The house was actually vibrating.

I got on my knees in the tub with the children, covering them with my arms. I told them not to listen to the noise, but to listen to me. I thought to myself, *We are going to die!* I thought about my grown daughter in California and hated to think of her being left alone if we died.

I started praying and asked for assistance. I prayed, *Please make this tornado go up and over this house now*. Then

I mentally affirmed, *We are protected. We are loved and protected now.* I asked my mother, who had passed on, to help us. I told myself, *We are not going to die; we are going to live.* The louder the noise, the louder I prayed. The noise was unbelievable, and the shaking was tremendous, but then it slowly subsided. When it seemed safe, I looked out the window, and all you could see was green fog. We were all alive and unhurt! It had passed.

Unfortunately, my neighbors were not so lucky. There was a total of six tornados at 7 P.M. that day in Allison. Nine people were killed, and many homes were destroyed. Part of my roof had been taken off, a brass bed had been thrown completely over our house, and the hubcaps on my car were sucked off. There were many houses where only the foundation still stood. Many people were in church that Sunday at that time of day, and they came home to find their houses gone. We did not have electricity or water for days, but we were alive.

A man came to me and said he saw the tornado sitting on my house like a hat, and he was sure we were all dead. Then he said it just took off up into the air. He said it was a miracle. It *was*—we were assisted by God and the angels. Another man saw the tornado hit our house, and he was sure we had all perished.

This experience changed my life. I believe in prayer and know that you only need to ask. As for the children in the tub, I doubt if they will ever forget it, and they now know the power of prayer as well as the importance of asking for protection.

۝۝۝

Lost and Found
by Bonnie Suzanne Koester

I had taken both of my daughters and their friends out to dinner to celebrate my oldest daughter's birthday. The restaurant is situated on the Houston Ship Channel and has a large lawn in between the water and the building. We had a great meal, and after dinner, the girls ran and frolicked on the lawn before we left. As soon as we got into the car, my daughter's friend exclaimed that she had lost her wallet with her driver's license in it. The girls all piled out of the car and started searching the lawn. It was very dark, so I parked the car so the headlights would shine on the lawn for them. It looked hopeless, like finding a needle in a haystack. As I sat in the car, I relaxed and asked my angels if they would please show me where the wallet was. I then saw a vision clearly in my mind's eye. I saw the wallet behind me, beside the backseat, near the door. I got out of the car and opened the back door, fully expecting to see the wallet—that's how clear the vision had been. But I couldn't see it. It was dark as pitch. I leaned closer, and then I saw a small glint of metal. I reached out, and it was the wallet! It was exactly where I'd envisioned it, even though I couldn't see it with my physical eyes. That was weird and really cool!

❦❦❦

Look What the Angels Dragged In!
by Carol Czerniec

A few years ago, I worked full-time, and my two children went to day care. My five-year-old son had a cat that he loved very much. She was very fat and declawed, and we always kept her in the house. But occasionally, she would sneak out and hide under the juniper bushes. The bushes were so sharp, sticky, and low to the ground that it was impossible to get her out.

One morning, I had the kids in the car ready to go, and I had to run back into the house for something I forgot. Sure enough, that cat ran out of the house and into the bushes. We were already late, and I knew from experience that it would take hours to get her out. I couldn't leave her there all day and risk something happening to her. My son would never forgive me!

I almost cried in despair, but instead I prayed to the angels to bring her back in. I stood there holding the door open, waiting for the angels to help me. Immediately, she came out from under the bushes. She was walking very strangely, very stiff like a puppet, with her eyes looking wild. She ran right in the front door without hesitating, and I shut it behind her. I couldn't see the angels dragging her in, but both the cat and I knew they were there!

❁❁❁

A Comforting Message
by Anonymous

It was a particularly difficult time for me. I had been divorced about eight years, my sons were off in college, and I was in graduate school. I felt isolated, lonely, and fearful. As I walked along the beach in the Cape Cod town where I lived, I tried to apply a nursing theory that I was studying to my life. The Betty Neumann System Theory states that if any one variable in a person's life is disrupted, the person is at risk of illness. An evaluation of me revealed an overweight, out-of-shape, isolated, and spiritually deprived woman.

As I thought about my status, I kept thinking of the influence that my early life was having on my current life.

My Dad, Richard Williamson, had been a wonderful man when he was sober. When he drank, though, he became a monster, abusing my mother and frightening my three older sisters and me. Dad died when I was seven, adding to my feelings of loss, abandonment, and anger.

I couldn't help but resent the effect my father's alcoholism had on my psychological development. However, I decided that day on the beach to make changes in my life for my general well-being. I decided to go on a diet, walk more often, and return to church. We had always been devout Catholics, but after my divorce, I felt abandoned, even by God, so I had given up any religious affiliation.

The next morning, I got up early for church. I had a good, healthy breakfast and began reading a magazine with my coffee. There was an article about a medium who communicated with people who had passed on to another plane. I never doubted that there was life after death, so I was not as skeptical as many of my friends would have been about the communications she described. I sort of laughingly said out loud to the room, "If my father is around me, he has a lot of making up to do!"

I went on to Mass. During each Mass, there comes a time where we pray for those who have died. You can imagine my reaction when the priest said, "We pray for all who have died, especially for Richard Williamson, for whom this Mass is being said." I felt a rush so strong that I turned around to see if someone had pushed me. There was no one close enough to have done so. I was so stunned by the mention of my father's name (even if there was another Richard Williamson in the area) so soon after I sent off my spoken message to him! The possibility of this being a coincidence does not exist for me. I know that my dad is able to see me and knows what's going on in my life, and that God allowed me to receive this reassuring message.

I'm now going to Overeaters Anonymous and am working with my angels daily. Dad's heavenly message and my angels are helping me to change my life from victimhood to victory!

❦❦❦

My Healing Angels
by Paige

For the past year, I've been going through a very emotional and draining lawsuit against my former employer. During the lawsuit, I've felt like everyone around me has betrayed me. As a result, I was left with only one true friend and a terrible feeling of loneliness. I went to a doctor about my depression, and he told me that I'd had an undiagnosed bipolar disorder for many years. He prescribed a simple antidepressant, which proved to be ineffective. So I tried to return to the doctor to get a stronger prescription, but since I had left my employment during the lawsuit, I no longer had health insurance.

Every day that bipolar disorder goes untreated is increasingly difficult. When you feel this depressed, hopeless, and alone, your thoughts shift to suicide. I was crying every day, all day! I was always wishing for death or thinking about how to put myself out of this misery. I started to drink to relieve my pain, and I never left my house. I did not have anything positive to hold on to in my life.

Well, my roommate's boss bought an angel book for her, which she gave me to read. I began talking to my angels every night before going to bed. I also kept a little prayer to my angel under my pillow.

The day that I began working with the angels, I lost all desire for alcohol, and I haven't taken any tranquilizers or cried since. I'm amazed at how well I'm sleeping, too, thanks to the angels. Because of them, I haven't even thought about suicide or how bad my life is.

Last night about 20 minutes after I spoke to my angels, I had this overwhelming feeling of happiness for no reason. I felt good—out of nowhere! I felt like a new person. And there were no drugs involved, just my faith and belief in angels. They say everything happens for a reason, and it truly does. My room-mate brought that book to me just in time. My angels were talking to me and trying to reach me, and they did.

❦❦❦

Angelic Assistance
by Lissy Dunning

Early in the year 2000, I was traveling to an important meeting in Kalamazoo, Michigan. I was driving 70 miles an hour and was in the passing lane on Interstate 94 when suddenly my left front tire blew out. There was no way for me to get to the right side of the road. I was already passing a vehicle, and there was one behind me in my lane. I was very scared and shaken but somehow managed to get off the road.

I had no cell phone and was at least a quarter mile from any gas station. As I stood outside my car, trying to decide which exit to walk to, I noticed a lot of truck drivers going in the opposite direction. I looked up at the sky and prayed, "Lord, please let one of these truck drivers stop and help me!"

Within three minutes, a truck driver turned around and did stop. Not only did he move my car to the opposite side of the road, but he also changed my tire and didn't charge me a thing. To me, this is one of the most incredible things I have been through. I was safe, and I got help quickly from above.

God and my guardian angels did double duty that day, and they worked better than a cell phone!

WWW

Confirmation from the Angels
by Gillian Holland

Having bought Doreen Virtue's book *Angel Visions* today, I ran myself a bath and slid into it, eager to relax and enjoy the read. After quite a while, the bathwater started getting cold. I then closed the book and asked to be given some confirmation of what I was reading, letting the book fall open all by itself. The page it opened to was page 144, an article by Marie Nelson called "Instant Validation." How's that for confirmation!

◗€ ◗€ ◗€

CHAPTER NINE

Angelic Protection

A Dream That Saved My Life
by Jill Wellington Schaeff

Armed with a journalism degree from Ohio State University, I was thrilled to land a job at a tiny radio station in Racine, Wisconsin, back in 1979. The hours were grueling, as I was covering evening city council meetings, and then I was up at three in the morning to report the morning-drive news on the air. All this for a paltry paycheck.

After ten months of little sleep, Andy, one of the disc jockeys, asked if I'd join him in a move to a bigger station in Evansville, Indiana. Wow—a raise and a bigger market! I was really on my way at the age of 23.

Five weeks later, Andy and I were fired. The station switched to automation, and the humans became obsolete. Andy easily landed another job in Evansville, but I did not. I started to get really worried when I scouted every station in town only to find that they had no news openings. Suddenly I missed my old job, friends, and that slim paycheck.

Andy offered to drive me back to Racine for a party weekend with the old gang. He said we could stay with his parents in nearby Milwaukee. I called my mother in Cincinnati and told her my plans. Not a half hour later she called me back.

"Grandma is in the hospital in bad shape. I'm going to Kenosha." Amazingly, Kenosha is just ten miles south of Racine. We planned to meet for dinner and go to the hospital together. What a strange, but nice, coincidence.

A violent thunderstorm pelted Kenosha when we arrived at the restaurant. It seemed to place a heavy pall over the meal. I was thrilled to be with my mother, but I felt vaguely depressed. She and Andy felt the same way, and we barely talked over dinner. But I remember that Mom asked Andy what his last name was several times.

When we arrived at the hospital, Grandma was sitting up in bed looking normal. We were confused by her spunk. She would be released the next day, and Mom wondered why she had made the long trip. I kissed her good-bye and went with Andy to attend a party with my former co-workers.

The party was a downer as well. Everyone was depressed. We couldn't put our finger on the lethargy. Andy came up to me several times to tell me that we had to leave his parents' house at 7:00 the next morning so he could make it back to Evansville for his first day at his new job. By 1:30 in the morning, I was exhausted.

"Let's get to my parents' house," Andy said. "We have to leave tomorrow at 7:00."

As I hugged everyone good-bye, various co-workers began to cry. One girl said, "Jill, we'll never see you again." That struck me as being wrong.

"I'll visit. Don't worry. We'll get together soon," I assured them. I couldn't figure out why everyone was acting so strange.

I was relieved to collapse into bed at Andy's house. I glanced at the clock. Two in the morning. I heard a knock on my door, and Andy's mother entered. "Your mother is on the phone."

I was certain something had happened to Grandma. Andy's mother ushered me to the phone in her bedroom. My mother was hysterical. "You can't leave with Andy tomorrow morning!" My mother had just experienced a vivid dream in bright color. A woman had come to the door and said, "Your daughter and my son were in a terrible accident. My son lived, but your daughter was killed!"

My mother sat up in bed and had a killer instinct to find me. She remembered asking Andy's last name at dinner, grabbed a phone book, and found the number. She said she would have stood out on the highway all night to stop me from making that trip.

I went to tell Andy we couldn't leave at 7:00. He looked pale and shaken. He, too, had felt a horrible dread about the trip. We realized that the whole weekend had been darkened with a sense of doom.

Andy left the next morning at 8:00 to break any chain that might have been in place for an accident. My mother drove from Kenosha to get me and drive me back to Evansville. When Andy's mother opened the door, my mother gasped. Andy's mother was the woman in her dream!

I know angels were working overtime that weekend, and I wasn't supposed to die at the age of 23. Whenever I'm down about something, I remember God's guidance. There are no coincidences. We are never alone.

❦❦❦

Lifted Out of Harm's Way
by Mary Jo Berlon

About ten years ago, I was walking with my two young children on the sidewalk of our subdivision in a suburb of

Cincinnati, Ohio. My children were about 15 feet ahead of me when I noticed a van backing into a driveway at the same time my preschooler was walking across it. The experience happened so fast that there was no earthly way my daughter could have moved out of the way of the van without Divine intervention.

Just as my daughter was crossing the driveway, I yelled, "No!" I stood amazed as I watched my daughter lifted from the driveway and plopped onto the front lawn! The van didn't touch her. She was fine! I hope that I remembered to thank her angels for helping her that day.

w/w/w

Angels Are Real
by Anonymous

I lived in a very small town in Missouri. I walked nearly everyplace I went because I didn't have a car. One afternoon I visited a friend. I stayed much later than I should have, and it got dark outside. I asked my friend to take me home, but she couldn't or wouldn't.

As a result, I had to walk down a two-lane highway at night. On the right side of this road was a one-foot walkway, and then about a three-foot drop-off into the grass. On the left was the same thing. In order to be seen by drivers, I thought it would be safest to walk down the road toward the middle. I saw headlights, and I moved to the one-foot side of the road.

Just then, I felt a large thump on my back, and a truck with wide side mirrors went past me. As I picked myself back up, I realized that I had been struck in the middle of my back by the truck. The truck was going at least 30 miles an hour when it hit me.

I know that an angel came between me and that truck. Otherwise, how can anyone account for the fact that I never even bruised and was not hurt in any way? Angels are real; they watch over us all the time.

)€)€)€

CHAPTER TEN

Angel Voices That Save Lives

Saved by a Voice
by Verlain Lane

It was winter, and the weather in Kansas was cold and clear that day. I had a medical appointment at the hospital two hours from our home.

My two-year-old son sat on the passenger side of our 1986 Toyota four-wheel-drive truck. I noticed that the sky was clouding over and getting dark, even though it had been sunny just an hour before when we left home. Before we got to the I-70 ramp, it was like a thick curtain suddenly fell in front of us.

I was surprised that the snow was coming down so fast and thick that I couldn't see anything. I slowed down and thought about turning around and going back home, but I kept going because I'd waited over two months for this appointment. Besides, we were almost halfway there, so I slowed down and we crept along until we got to the Interstate ramp, because I felt sure it would clear off any minute. But it didn't.

Shortly after heading east on I-70, I saw cars off the road everywhere, and 18-wheelers slowed to a crawl. I had locked in my four-wheel drive, and I told my little son we'd be okay.

I was coming up on an overpass bridge, and just as I hit the small drop-off seam of pavement, the Toyota skidded on the ice.

As it went into a skid, the last thing I saw was that my toddler had unfastened his seatbelt! I reached out with my right hand and grabbed his left wrist as I steered into the skid with my left hand. I couldn't bring it out of the skid, and I couldn't let go of my baby son.

I heard a male voice plainly say, "Hold on to the boy, let go of the wheel, and close your eyes." I didn't stop to think about who was talking to me; I just did it.

When I opened my eyes, a man jerked open my driver's door and asked if I was okay. Our Toyota had jumped the overpass railing and skidded along the entire length of the concrete rail as if it were on a track. I assured the stranger we were fine, and he said he'd call for help. Most miraculous of all was the fact that my pickup didn't have a single dent or scratch!

The first words out of my toddler's mouth were, "Wow, Mama!" as he clapped his hands. Waiting for help, I tried to figure out who had spoken those words when the truck skidded out of control. It was the most serene, controlled, masculine voice I'd ever heard. So calm and soothing. I remember doing as I was told, and a peaceful, loving feeling wrapped around me. It was as if my son and I were being held tightly in a giant hug.

We made it to my medical appointment, and when I told the doctor (who was a golfing buddy of our family priest) what had happened, he said, "You understand you met an angel today, don't you?" I could only nod.

Although it has been 14 years this month, I'll never forget the loving guidance spoken to me on that icy March morning.

⟪⟫⟪⟫⟪⟫

Arthur's Angel
by Jenny Leamon

Rushing to work one day, I heard a clear voice say, "Slow down," so I did. About a mile up the road, an elderly man who was riding a bicycle was hit by the car in front of me. The bike and its rider fell straight in front of me. Because I obeyed the voice, I had time to stop without harming the man.

I talked to the man, who told me that his name was Arthur. Arthur said that he'd had seven experiences of Divine intervention since his sister had passed away the previous year. Arthur had been extremely close to his sister, and he knew she was his angel that day. Sometimes I think that Arthur was an angel to *me* because of what I learned from this experience.

ఆఆఆఆ

Thank God for the Angels
by Rebecca Thrasher

I was driving home from work early, feeling over-whelmed. My youngest son, Tyler, was home sick, and I was getting married the next day. I felt totally unprepared. If that wasn't enough, I had company coming to my house for the wedding.

Tyler's doctor had said that he had a virus, and all day long, my son had called me to say that he felt increasingly worse. I wondered if I needed to take him to the urgent-care center. I called his doctor, who said it was part of my son's virus. I wondered, *Should I take Tyler to the medical center anyway?* I didn't want to take any chances with my son's health. But on the other hand, I had so many things to do that night, and the doctor had reassured me that Tyler's health was normal.

That was when I heard a voice say, "It's his appendix!" in a loud and stern way. So I took Tyler to the clinic. The doctor began telling me that he thought it was the virus, but I said I just wanted to be sure it wasn't his appendix. He did another exam and went to get another doctor who did the same thing. They then sent us to the hospital to see a surgeon. Tyler had his appendix removed that night just before it burst. I thank God and His angels for saving my son's life.

❦❦❦

Keeping Me Safe
by Diane Smith

One morning around 5:30 A.M. while driving to work, I was on a road where there were woods and no lights other than car headlights. All of a sudden, I heard a voice telling me to start putting my brakes on. I did, and out of the woods a large deer appeared right in front of my car.

When I started to drive again, I heard the same voice telling me not to because there was another deer. I stopped again, and out of the woods came another large deer.

If I had not listened to this voice both times, I would have hit the deer and probably injured myself, too. I know this was my guardian angel keeping me safe. This was really the first time I had heard my guardian angel, and now whenever I hear that voice, I listen.

❦❦❦

The Angel of White Light
by Jim St. Onge

The weather was a mess in New England that day. Snow, sleet, freezing rain. Yuck! I was out on an errand and found the road conditions worsening as I made my way home. Up ahead in the distance, I could see two police cars and a car that had crashed into a telephone pole.

I slowed down, but my car began sliding and heading toward the other cars. I quickly visualized my car being surrounded by white light, and I mentally yelled for the angels to bring the car under control. All of a sudden, I heard a voice say, *Take your foot off the brake!*

I obeyed the instruction, and the car, which was about to lose control, slowed miraculously and stopped just before I would have crashed into a police car. As I slowly drove by the accident scene, I sent many angels to this woman, who seemed to be unhurt, thank God.

I give my angels much thanks for their help in this situation. The angels saved me from potential injuries!

❧❧❧❧

"Slow Down!"
by Arlene Martin

I jog in the evenings along Lake Michigan. One night as I was running, a "voice " told me to slow down my run. I didn't listen. I started to jog a few feet, and my pedometer quit working. I stopped jogging in order to reset it. When I returned to jogging, I again heard the voice tell me to slow down. I ignored the voice, and again, my pedometer stopped working. I slowed down so I could reset the pedometer, and I continued my jog at a slower pace.

A few minutes later, right in front of where I was jogging, an accident occurred between two cars. One of the cars became airborne and landed about six yards directly in front of me, right on the jogging pathway. Had I not slowed down, I would have been hit by the car. To this day, *I know* it was my angel.

❦❦❦

Thank God I Listened
by Debbie Hoskin

My son, Jason, had just gotten his driving permit. It was a Sunday afternoon, and he asked if we could go driving. I thought it would be a great way to spend some quality time with him, so I agreed and let him drive. We had been driving for approximately 20 minutes down a country highway. Jason was doing a great job, so I began to relax and look at the scenery. Actually, I became very relaxed and forgot that my inexperienced 17-year-old son was at the wheel.

Suddenly something told me to stop daydreaming. It said, *Pay attention to your son driving.* Then, like a vivid daydream, I saw a flash or vision of a red car coming around the bend at us in our lane. I almost didn't pay attention to it, but I gave in to a strong feeling to give instructions to my son on what to do in the event of a potential head-on collision. He listened carefully and repeated the instructions back to me.

Within a minute, a small red car came speeding around the bend of the highway, passing a slower-moving vehicle heading toward us in our lane. My son knew exactly what to do to prevent what might have been a fatal accident. I knew that we had been warned by a guardian angel. I expressed my gratitude many times that day and vowed to always trust my intuition.

❦❦❦

Rescued by an Earth Angel
by Lorein Cipriano

I was driving on Route 8 from Torrington, Connecticut, after visiting a friend in Waterbury, where I live. It was late, around one o'clock in the morning. The road was very dark.

Suddenly, I saw a car parked on the side of the road. A voice said to me, "Stop! Stop!" Ordinarily, I would never stop on a dark road like this, but the voice created such an urgency in me that I slammed on the brakes and pulled over in front of the car.

I looked back and saw a woman jump out of the passenger seat of the car, and she started running toward mine. The driver of her car, a man, also got out. The woman approached the front passenger side of my car. And the voice came again: "Let her in!"

I opened the passenger door, and the woman, who was crying, got in. The man then came around my side of the car and started banging on the window. The voice said, "Go!" So I put my foot on the gas and sped away as fast as I could. The woman told me that she'd been working late at a factory, but the person who was supposed to pick her up to take her home didn't show up, and this man (who worked in the same factory) offered her a lift.

However, on the way home, he had stopped the car and tried to sexually molest her. She was trying to fight him off when my car pulled over in front of them. She was grateful, to say the least, and I attribute this to the help of her angels, and mine. I truly believe that God speaks to us and guides us through His angels.

❦❦❦

A Lifesaving Warning
by Jane Anne Morgan

Last year I was awakened by the sound of my CO_2 detector (a device that detects gas leaks) beeping. Earlier that week, my neighbor who shared the duplex next to my wall had experienced a similar situation. It turned out that both of our CO_2 detectors had malfunctioned within the same week.

Anyway, I was so sleepy that night that I got out of bed to unplug the detector to stop its beeping. I thought I would check on it in the morning when I was awake. Just then, though, the telephone rang. As I picked up the receiver, I heard a recorded voice say, "You have a collect call from . . ." and then a really deep and watery voice said, "You're orange," with these two words stretched out slowly.

The moment that I heard these words, I had an inner knowing: "I left my gas oven on!" When gas is dangerous, the flame burns orange. I ran to the kitchen, where I discovered that— yes, I had left the gas oven turned on. So my CO_2 detector wasn't malfunctioning; it was correctly warning me. I probably would have been dead within two hours if the phone call hadn't warned me of danger.

But where did that phone call come from? Since it was a collect call, I waited until my phone bill arrived in the mail so I would have a record of the call's origination number. The phone bill showed that the call had come in at 4:45 A.M. from a place in Dennison, Texas. I live in Oklahoma.

I called the number, and it was a place called The Cardinal Motel. The manager said there was no way to know who had placed the call that night. How would they know about my gas oven? Whoever called me that night saved my life, and I believe that it was an angel.

Saved by My Guardian Angel
by Alison Clarke Taylor

I was about 20 years old and I was returning to my home on a very narrow, winding country road. This road wound around trees and up over a blind hill. I always approached this hill with caution and stayed far to the right. However, there were vertical banks on each side of this narrow road, so there wasn't much room for two cars to pass.

One day, just as I approached this hill, I heard a voice say, "Pull over and stop." I was alone in the car. I felt the steering wheel being turned to the right, so I obeyed the voice. I sat there for about two seconds wondering why I had stopped—something that I had never done in the hundreds of times that I had negotiated that road.

Just as I was contemplating why I had pulled over, a woman roared over the hill in a large car, going very, very fast and completely taking up the road. I would have probably been killed or very critically injured if I'd had a head-on collision with this car. I feel that my life was saved that day by my guardian angel.

❀❀❀

An Urgent Message
by Denise Jones

When I was ten years old, my tonsils ruptured, and I was very sick and having trouble breathing. My mother decided to put an electrical facial sauna beside my bed and direct the steam to my face in the hopes that it would make breathing easier for me. She took some newspaper and laid it over the facial sauna and then over my face, to direct the steam toward me.

My bed was pushed up against the wall, but I felt someone crawl into my bed between me and the wall. I was happy, because I thought it was my mother who had come to lie down with me. I turned my face toward the wall to tell her "Hi," and then I realized that I could not see anyone there. Yet, there was a definite weight pressing against my right side.

Then I heard a man's voice say in my right ear: "Turn your face to the wall and the paper will save your face." I said out loud, "No. I'm just afraid that the facial sauna is boiling dry, and I know that my mom will be in here any minute to get it."

I continued to lie there, and the voice said a second time, a little more urgently this time: "Turn your face to the wall, and the paper will save your face." Again, I argued that I would be fine and would wait for my mom to return. All of a sudden, he screamed in my ear, with the loudest sound that I have ever heard: "TURN YOUR FACE TO THE WALL NOW!"

At that second, I flipped my body toward the wall and my shoulder pulled the paper off the facial sauna. That was also the second that three feet of fire shot up out of the facial sauna just as my mother stepped into the room. If the newspaper had caught on fire, I would not have been able to move it fast enough to keep my face from being burned.

I told my mom that I knew something was going to happen and about the man who had been in bed with me. She told me to always listen to that voice because it's my guardian angel, and he's there to protect and guide me. That was my first up-close and personal experience with him, and it changed my life. I sense him around me all the time and feel so comfortable when he talks to me.

❦❦❦

The Nurse Who Talks to Angels
by Anonymous

I'm a nurse who was working at Stanford Hospital on the night shift in 1989. The only way for me to handle the monthly day/night rotations was to pray before I went into work, since I was sometimes working for 24 hours at a time. I prayed for Divine assistance that I could get through the night, and that I would be safe and alert for anything that arose.

One particular night while I was walking into a patient's room, I heard a voice tell me to go down the opposite end of the hall and check on another patient of mine. I thought to myself, *I just checked on him not too long ago, and he was sleeping and doing fine.* Normally, the nightly rounds on every patient occurred every two hours, and I had just seen that patient about 45 minutes prior.

I contemplated the voice, trying to rationalize, *But I just saw him*, and yet the voice persisted. I then decided, *Okay, I'll go check on him.* I put down the other patients' medications and walked all the way down the long hallway and into this patient's room. He was sleeping, so I put my hand on his chest, asking if he was all right. As my hand touched him, I noticed something wet, so I turned on the light. I then noticed he was hemorrhaging from a central line site where the line had been taken out by the prior shift hours before!

I immediately applied a pressure dressing. I asked the patient if he felt any pain or knew he was bleeding, and he said no. He was dreaming away! I then knew that the only way for me to have caught this hemorrhaging in the beginning was due to Divine guidance. I was very thankful, and now I really listen to the guidance of my angels.

❦❦❦

Angel Guidance Kept Me Safe
by Martin W. Acevedo

One evening in March of 1997, I didn't get home until bed-time. I was very tired and looking forward to resting. When I walked in the door, I heard a voice say in a straightforward man-ner: "Don't go to bed yet." It was neither a feminine nor mas-culine voice, and it wasn't menacing or sweet. It was simply a calm instruction.

I am an elder of a church that honors the spiritual beliefs of the East and West and was raised praying for the assistance of the angels, so this communique did not seem unusual to me. I simply said out loud, "Okay," and kept myself occu-pied in the living room for a while. Soon, I sensed that what-ever was going to happen would happen soon. At that moment, I heard an intermittent buzzing sound coming from my kitchen.

I walked into the kitchen and saw that the electrical out-let for my refrigerator had caught on fire, and the flames were spreading up the kitchen wall! I was renting an older home at the time, and the outlet or wiring was probably worn out. I could only think, *Wow,* knowing why I had received so time-ly a message, and put out the fire with a small kitchen extin-guisher that I kept nearby.

Thinking about the episode later, I said happily to my unseen friend, "Thank you." Later, as I walked toward my bedroom, I received one more message from my guardian angel: "Check your smoke detector."

I reached up and tested the smoke detector near my bed-room and discovered that the battery was dead. Had I not been attuned to my guardian angel's message, I probably would have died from the kitchen fire as well.

I am very grateful for the partnership that exists between

heaven and earth, so that we each can fulfill our sacred missions here. I hope this inspires others to be open to their angel friends.

ʬʬʬ

Angels Watching Over Me
by Azaya Deuel

My first angel experience happened when I was around four years old. My brothers, Bobby and Billy, and my sister, Anne, and I were at a park in Azusa, California, near our home. While my siblings played with friends at one end of the park, I wandered to the fountain at the other end.

A man approached me and asked if I wanted some candy. I asked if I could have some for my brothers and sister, too. He said yes and told me to follow him behind one of the buildings by the parking lot and he would give me all the candy I wanted. I was intent on going with him because I really wanted some candy.

As I started to follow him, though, I heard a voice say, "You have to go tell your brothers and sister where you're going." I repeated what I'd heard to the man, but he tried to tell me that it wasn't necessary and that we'd only be gone a few minutes. I kept insisting that I had to tell them, and then I did as I was directed and got my brother Billy's attention. He called from across the park and asked where I was going. I told him I was going with the nice man to get some candy for all of us. I turned around to find the man gone. The other kids came running and checked the parking lot, but the man was nowhere to be found. They kept me close by after that.

Later that night, the police came to our house and asked a lot of questions. It was during a time when there were a lot of kidnapings, in late 1949. Fortunately, my angel intervened, and even more fortunately, I listened and obeyed!

❧❧❧

On the Wings of Angels
by Azaya Deuel

My husband, Dan, was a pilot and flight instructor who owned his own plane. One day, Dan and I went flying from an airport in La Verne, California, and headed over the Big Bear mountains of Southern California. It was an incredibly beautiful day, and everything was going well. Suddenly, the plane's engine started to sputter and quit.

Dan tried everything he could think of, but nothing helped, so he started looking for a place to crash land. Things weren't looking too good. I knew nothing about airplanes, and Dan never talked to me about airplanes or their mechanics. I actually saw my life flash before my eyes, like you read about in books.

Then I heard a voice say, "Carb heat. Tell him to pull the carb heat," so I did. I yelled, "Carb heat! Pull on the carb heat!" I guess it shocked Dan enough that he immediately pulled on the carburetor heat knob.

I'm sure all of this took place in a matter of seconds or minutes, but it seemed like an eternity. Pulling on the carb heat worked, and we were able to get to the airport and land safely!

As Dan explained to me later, the carburetor had iced up during storms that occurred over the previous days, and the ice prevented the engine from receiving fuel. Once the situation was under control, Dan just looked at me and said, "How?" I told him about the angel's voice. I don't think he believed me, but I knew without a doubt that the angels were flying with our airplane that day, and that they'd just saved our lives!

❅ ❅ ❅

CHAPTER ELEVEN

Angel Voices of Comfort and Guidance

"Everything Is Going According to Plan"
by Ruth Winocur

It was a time of great loss in my life. My mother had just passed away, and six weeks later, my husband died after having a massive heart attack. I was left high and dry, without anyone.

One evening, while weeping, I heard a voice in my head say, "Why are you weeping? Everything is going according to plan. There is no reason to weep, but you may do so if it makes you feel better." That was all that was said, but it did turn out to be a major turning point in my life.

❦❦❦

"It Is Not Time Yet"
by Anonymous

I was involved in a car accident where my body was thrown out of my car. At the point of impact, time slowed down and my mind became calm and clear. As I flew out of my car, I landed first on my head and neck, bounced and flipped through the air, and then landed on my tailbone in a sitting position in oncoming traffic. I did not feel any of this. In fact, I felt as if I were in a cocoon or bubble with lots of light.

As I was going through this, I asked the question, "Am I going to die?" I was answered with "No. It is not time yet."

I had no broken bones or internal injuries. I know that my guardian angels were there protecting me.

❦❦❦

"Be Loving and Kind to Everyone!"
by Irene Weinberg

It had been a grueling month filled with business upsets. My husband, Saul, and I had finally escaped to our weekend getaway in the mountains to ski and relax. We were on our way home when Saul fell asleep at the wheel. I saw the look of concern that crossed his face in the moment he awoke and tried to pull our car out of its swerve. As the car flipped over and rolled down the embankment, I somehow knew, from a place deep within me, that Saul was gone.

Even though I was covered by a blanket, I shivered as I was put on a stretcher, loaded into a helicopter, and flown to an Emergency Trauma Center. Throughout this tragedy, I was able to maintain a strength and serenity that astounded me. This was because of the heavenly messages I received before and during the accident.

Two months before Saul died, while I was working in my kitchen, I heard an inner voice say, "Saul has to go. He has touched many lives, and many lessons will be learned from his death." I shuddered at these words and pushed them away from me. How could I even *think* such a thing?

Yet, during the accident, I heard a very definite, clear voice in my head say, "He's not going to make it. You are."

It felt like a thought of my own, expressed with a great knowing, yet it also seemed to come from a place outside of me. When our car hit the ground, we rolled down an embankment four times before we landed. But then I felt the car being turned over, and as I was pulled out of the window by very strong hands, I heard yet another message: "Be loving and kind to everyone!"

This message flooded my being with the authority of a directive. Its "voice " had a decidedly masculine tone to it, and there was absolutely no doubt in my mind that this message came from outside of me. The last thing that would be on my mind, as my badly injured body was being taken from a car that now held my dead husband, was "Be loving and kind to everyone!"

This last message resonated deep within me, strongly signaling me that something incredible and unearthly was happening. Saul was supposed to go . . . and I was supposed to go on. This was meant to be.

Before our tragic accident, Saul and I were highly skeptical of all things spiritual. We thought you had to be crazy to believe in that stuff. But after the accident and the messages I received, I was transformed.

❦❦❦

A Message of Comfort
by Pam Davis

I was absolutely distraught. It was three weeks after my baby son, Ryan, had passed away from Sudden Infant Death Syndrome. I had almost fallen asleep when I heard footsteps in my kitchen. They grew louder as they approached my bedroom.

But instead of seeing a person walking, I saw a green mist float around to the corner of my bedroom door. Naturally, I was frightened! Then I heard a voice that instantly calmed me down. It said that Ryan was okay and I would see him again in the outer world of heaven someday. Somehow that was enough to give me peace to go on.

I will never forget that experience. It was an event that gave me hope. I believe it was an angel that was trying to calm and ease my pain.

❦❦❦

My Best Friend, Raffy
by John Catalano

I was introduced to my good friend, Raffy, when I listened to Doreen's audiotape *Divine Guidance*. In the tape, when Doreen mentioned Archangel Raphael, he resonated with me, even though she mentioned several other angels. I found myself always thinking about him.

I began asking him for help during the day, and I always received his assistance. I began to refer to Archangel Raphael as "Raffy," and we developed a very close friendship. It's rare that more than a couple of hours pass in a day without him coming up in my mind. He has helped me so many times and in so many ways that I can't begin to tell you all the stories.

But something significant happened when I went to see a medium one day. As she started to do my reading, she looked at me in a confused kind of way. She said that there was someone here with me, and that he was *always* with me, but she couldn't determine who it was. Then, after a long pause, she said, "His name is Ralphy." I knew that she was referring to Raffy! He is my best friend, and I wake up every morning and go to bed every night feeling very fortunate to have him with me.

❦❦❦

Highway Angel
by LaurieJoy Pinkham

It was Tuesday, April 22, 1998, and I was driving to New York City to attend The Great Experiment prayer vigil at a church near the United Nations. As I drove over the hill, a state trooper pulled me over.

"Good morning, miss. Do you have any idea how fast you were going?"

"Sure I do. I set my cruise control for 62 miles an hour, just a little over the speed limit," I replied with a friendly smile.

"Madam, the speed limit through here is 40 miles per hour. You were going 22 over the limit!" he said indignantly.

"I had no idea. Where did the speed limit change?" I asked.

"Back at the flashing light. May I see your license and registration, please?"

I promptly retrieved my papers from the glove box.

"Miss, what does your driving record look like?" he asked. At that moment, a quiet voice in my heart spoke to me gently, like an angel. It said to me, "LaurieJoy, please give this man an *Emissary of Light* newsletter. Tell him about The Great Experiment. Tell him about the millions of people who will be meditating and praying for peace tomorrow."

Usually, I listen to this inner voice, but this request seemed outlandish, given the circumstances. The officer returned to my car, and as he handed me my papers, he said, "Because you were honest with me and because I think that you can find a better use for the money than this fine would cost you, I'm going to just give you a warning."

"What?" I questioned with total disbelief as tears of gratitude rolled down my cheeks. I reached across the seat, picked up a newsletter about the prayer vigil, and handed it to him, while explaining briefly what it was all about.

The officer smiled, thanked me, and waved as I drove away. Silently, I gave thanks to my angels.

Two weeks later, I was in the town hall and this same officer came up to me and said, "Thank you for the newsletter. I read it, bought the book, meditated with all of you, and felt that I was making a difference somehow. Thank you so very much. Whatever prompted you to give me that newsletter?"

I replied truthfully without hesitation, "The angels of the highway did—the ones that take care of each of us when we're out there doing what we need to do every single day. Thank you for the wonderful experience. I'm glad that you stopped me on that day."

We never know what each day will bring, who will enter our lives, or how we can make a small difference, even in times of adversity. We just never know. I do know that on that day, I was stopped to help another on his path, and he stopped me to help me understand just that.

❦❦❦❦

A Gift from Lou
by Cathy

I was shopping, and from out of nowhere I heard a message in my head that said, "Go to the cemetery." I dismissed the thought and continued to shop. Again, I heard the message, but this time much stronger: "Go to the cemetery today."

Okay, I mentally agreed. But then I asked myself, *What cemetery, and why am I going?* The answer I heard was: "Just drive to the cemetery."

So I drove to the closest cemetery, and as I drove through the gates, I saw five different roads. I had never been to this cemetery before, so I asked myself, "Where do I go?"

"Just drive," was the reply that I heard. I followed the

long and curvy roads until I heard the voice say, "Slow down." I read the headstones as I drove, but I still wasn't sure what I was looking for. Then I heard another message: "Lou." That was the name of my friend's father who had passed away 11 years ago. I had never met him.

I drove up and down the cemetery roads, but I couldn't locate Lou's grave, so I decided to go to the cemetery office. I gave them Lou's full name and asked if they could find his gravesite for me. They said that I would never be able to locate Lou's grave on my own, so one of the office personnel offered to drive to the site and have me follow her in my car.

I couldn't believe it when she took me back to the exact spot where I had been when the voice told me to "slow down."

I mentally laughed and asked Lou, "Why didn't you tell me to park the car and walk? I would have found you sooner." The peaceful feeling I had while I was there and after I left was unearthly. I just don't know how to describe it, but I'm glad that I experienced it by listening to the voice.

ɷɷɷ

Practical Advice from My Angel
by Sheila Wingert

I've only heard my guardian angel speak to me once, and that was a long time ago. I was studying one of my college nursing books, and out of the blue I heard a voice say, "Check your tire." It was my first time hearing my angel so strongly. I just ignored the voice, thinking that it didn't make any sense. But the next day after class, I came out to the parking lot and found that I had a flat tire. I haven't been able to hear my angel since then, but I feel his presence with me all the time now.

ӬЄ ӬЄ ӬЄ

CHAPTER TWELVE

Voices of Deceased Loved Ones

Pet Reunion
by Patricia Genetos

My father passed away very recently. Right before Dad died, I asked him to let me know he was okay. Unexpectedly, though, I became frightened as I lay in bed that night at my brother's house, where Dad had suffered and died in the room downstairs.

The next thing I knew, I felt drowsy, and a pleasant wave of peacefulness came over me, flowing from my toes to my head. I then had a feeling of great joy and heard these six words: "I found Misty. How about that?" It was my father!

Dad had reunited with his beloved little white dog, Misty, in heaven. He knew that I, being quite an animal lover, would relate to what he told me. I smiled and went peacefully to sleep.

❦❦❦

A Promise of Love
by Laura M. Mehlhorn

When I was 19 years old, my Great-Uncle Jim was dying of cancer after years of smoking. The doctors had informed him that he only had a few months left before he would be too ill to travel and would die sedated and in terrible pain.

He wanted to see all of the family one last time before he got too ill. During that last visit, he put his hands on my shoulders, looked me intently in the eyes, and said, "I want you to make me a solemn promise, so don't make it unless you intend to keep it. This is a promise to a dying man, so it's sacred. Promise me that you will never smoke, never even put a cigarette to your lips." He didn't want to have anyone else go through what he was enduring.

Neither of my parents smoked, and I had not yet felt tempted to try it, so I thought it would be an easy promise to keep. I promised him, with loving tears in my eyes, that I wouldn't smoke.

About four years later, I was spending an evening with my fiancé and some of his friends. One of the friends, a smoker himself, suggested that I at least try a cigarette since I never had. I had forgotten my promise. As I held the offered cigarette between my fingers and considered having it lit, I felt warm hands on my shoulders and a voice that held such a magnitude of disappointment in it. The words were simply: "Oh, but honey, you promised!"

That was all I needed to hear. I instantly knew who was speaking to me, and I remembered the promise. I dropped the cigarette without ever having touched it to my lips, and I've never forgotten the promise again. I am now 53 years old and have a healthy pair of lungs—thanks to my loving great-uncle.

Grandpa's Loving Voice
by Candice Graham

I was reading [psychic medium] John Edward's book, *One Last Time*, and was very intrigued by its content. I was coming back from Florida and was sitting next to my husband on the plane. In the back of the book, there's a meditation you can do to get relaxed enough to have possible contact with someone who has died and gone to the Other Side.

So I tried it, but at the end of the meditation, I thought, *Well, this is not working for me; maybe it's because I'm on a plane with so many people around.* At that very moment, I heard my grandpa's voice, clear as a bell! He said, "I love you, honey!" Tears welled up behind my eyes and rushed down my face.

I was so relieved because I knew it was him. And it wasn't scary, like I thought it might have been. It was him, his same voice, with the exact same timbre, and the exact same way he would say it. I have to tell you, it was fantastic. I just said, "I love you, too, Grandpa."

Grandpa was a very religious Christian who went to a strict church where they didn't believe in talking to the dead. So it's ironic that he talked to me from heaven. I believe if you want to contact someone with all your heart and have the love of God in mind, it can be as wonderful as the day they were here.

One of the reasons that this story is so important to me is that for years I have longed for a validation that heaven really exists. After Grandpa passed, I prayed so hard, "Oh, God, please let there be a heaven that Grandpa is going to." Now I know for certain that heaven truly exists, and that Grandpa is home where he belongs.

❧ ❧ ❧

CHAPTER THIRTEEN

The Sounds of Angels

They Saved My Life That Night
by Sheryl S. Soper

I was driving home from my boyfriend's home late at night. I was very tired and fell asleep at the wheel. The next thing I knew, someone was screaming my name and pulling my hair. I woke up and saw that I was headed toward a cement wall that was in a *V* shape where the highway split in two.

I just missed that wall and knew that my angels were responsible for waking me up. They saved my life that night! I am always sure to say thank you to my angels.

❧❧❧

Instant Believer
by Sandra Leal

This story is about my husband, who was not a believer until this happened. I always pray to God and the angels, but he never believed in angels. He says that this event made him a believer in 20 short seconds.

My husband travels a lot with his job and drives in difficult terrain all the time. He was driving along a narrow mountain road when suddenly he looked down and saw sunflower seeds, which he rarely, if ever, eats while driving. He opened his window (which he never does) to get rid of the seeds, and suddenly heard a cry for help. The plea was very loud, and he heard it several times. He stopped his vehicle and backed up because he thought someone had fallen down the side of the mountain.

Just as he stopped, a very large boulder landed right in the road where he would have been. He got out of his vehicle and realized that had he not backed up, he would have been killed. We can't explain this other than that an angel saved his life.

✺✺✺

Wide Awake
by Fred Lehmann

Many years ago as I drove through Kansas on a long road trip, I was very tired, so I turned on my eight-track tape of the *Grassroots Greatest Hits* to help keep me awake.

I dozed off at the wheel but was abruptly awakened when I heard a loud scream that seemed to come from the tape. I'm sure the scream saved my life.

Afterward, I listened to the same song again, but there was no scream. So it had to have been my guardian angel warning me of danger. There is no other explanation for what woke me.

✺✺✺

And the Angels Sang
by Susan

In November of 1995, I was living far away from my family. In the middle of the night, I was slowly awakened by beautiful singing. It sounded like a female voice, singing progressively higher-pitched notes. I was now wide awake, but not at all afraid. Then, the last note was even more high-pitched, with a sense of lightness to it. The music crescendoed and then disappeared into the air.

Since the music sounded like it had come from the living room, I got up and began looking behind all the doors, trying to discover the source of the music. But there was nothing! The next morning, my family called me to say that my grandmother had passed away during the night.

❦❦❦

A Noise That Saved My Life
by Brenda Gagas

A guardian angel guided me home safely from college one day. The year was 1991, mid-September. I didn't get much sleep the night before driving home for my sister's wedding. I was tired, exhausted from a night of tossing and turning, with thoughts racing through my head. The drive was over four hours through the Upper Peninsula of Michigan and northern Wisconsin. About two hours into the drive on a two-lane highway, I found myself wanting to take long blinks to rest my eyes. It never occurred to me what would happen if I fell asleep at the wheel.

One long blink ended abruptly with a "thud"on the windshield. I opened my eyes wide, quickly looking to see what

I had hit. There was nothing—no marks on the windshield in front of the passenger seat where the noise had come from, no debris flying in the air or rolling on the highway. I knew at that moment that the sound was different from hitting some object. The sound had too much solid force behind it, just as if someone had pounded their fist on the windshield. I looked in amazement at the passenger seat, knowing in my heart that God had sent an angel to wake me from an accident that could have taken my life and more.

Well, the blood and adrenaline rushing through my body did not last long enough to keep me awake for long. Within 30 minutes, I felt very tired again. I tried opening the windows and playing the radio loud. But my eyes still wanted to close themselves into a deep sleep while my car hurtled along at 60 miles an hour.

Before I knew it, another "thud" pounded my car. This time, cars were passing by me, and there was a slight curve in the road ahead. My eyes wide open once again, with my heart pounding heavily, I looked in my mirrors to see what had hit me. Nothing. The "thud" came from the left front fender, above my front tire. This time I was wide awake, praying, and thanking God and my guardian protector. I knew I was not alone. I couldn't see anything, but I still know to this day that a guardian angel was sitting on the hood of my car, guiding me home safely. In all my life, I have never heard a "thud"on my car or any car I was a passenger in. Since then, I have never needed to rest my eyes while driving.

❧ ❧ ❧

CHAPTER FOURTEEN

Sensing an Angel or Deceased Loved One Through Touch or Scent

Thank You, Great-Grandma!
by Tracey Staples

When my great-grandmother passed away, I was devastated. She was my best friend, and I always felt a special connection with her. She always knew the right thing to say to make me feel better about everything when no one else could.

I couldn't believe she was gone. I think I really worried my mother because I refused to believe it. I would always have these very "real" dreams about spending time with her. Now I know that I actually was spending time with her in my dream state.

But one day I finally realized that she was dead. I was listening to the Barry Manilow song "Can't Smile Without You," and the words just struck me. I wept for days, just as I did right after she passed. The pain and grief were unbearable. On top of my grief, I was deeply panicked and depressed about finding a place to move to. I couldn't bear the thought that she was no longer there to make it better!

A couple of days later, I was at the theater watching a movie. In the middle of the film, I suddenly felt this draft of cold air. When I took breaths, I could smell my great-grandmother. It was a very surreal experience. I was freaked out, but at the same time felt this overwhelming feeling of joy. I looked around the theater to see if there was any other way to explain the draft of cold air, and there wasn't any.

There was no way I could explain the scent, because my great-grandmother always smelled of whatever powder she wore, with Ben-Gay blended in. It was a very unique smell! After the incident, I did not smell it at all. I'm someone who always notices details about people—the way they smell, all of their physical features, and how I feel when I'm around them. So my memory of Great-Grandma's smell is very keen, and I'm certain that it was the same one that I sensed in the theater.

All the way home, I was shocked as well as joyful that it had all happened. It was almost like time stood still afterward, and I had this euphoric feeling. I was so pleased that Great-Grandma let me know she was there.

On Tuesday of that week, my mother called me and said that for some reason she was late for work (which is very unusual for her). Then as she walked out of the apartment building, she ran into the landlord. Now, she hadn't run into the landlord in the whole year she had been living there.

My mother told the landlord that I needed my own place to live, and she said that they had one new vacancy. My mother told me, "Now, Tracey, if this isn't a sign you should move into this building, then I don't know what is!" I called the landlord, and I was able to move into the apartment right away. She even allowed me to pay the deposit in installment payments. Thank you for your help, Great-Grandma!

❀❀❀

Flying Through the Stars
by Paulina Tito

I was sleeping, and suddenly in the middle of the night, I woke up but fell asleep again. The next thing I knew, I was in a dark, peaceful place. Behind me, I could feel my angel. I couldn't really see her, but I knew that it was my guardian angel and that she had taken me to the stars. We started to play, and she made me laugh like I was a little girl again!

We were flying around the stars, and I knew that my angel was behind me, showing me the sense and beauty of flying. We were flying so fast that I felt the wind in my ears, and a kind of excitement that isn't possible to feel in life. She was going so fast that I had to tell her to slow down. But without talking, just by thinking of it, she instantly slowed down.

Then, I knew it was time to go back home, and in that instant, I opened my eyes. I felt so happy and my heart was beating so fast. I thanked my angel with all my heart, and I lit a candle in her honor.

※※※

He Kept His Promise
by Peggy L. Lorenz

My husband, Joe, passed away two and a half years ago after an eight-month bout with kidney cancer. We had a lot of time to talk about what my future would be like without him, what to do with our children, our business, and many of the little things that we wanted to settle before he passed on.

One of the things that we discussed at great length was our after-life. We're both Christians and believe that our eternity will be spent together with the Lord. But I had a request for my husband. For my own peace of mind, I asked that if there was any way that he could let me know that he was okay when he passed over, to please do so, so that I wouldn't worry about him. We were so connected in life that I knew that if he could do this for me, he would. I just had no idea how quickly it would happen.

Joe passed away at 3:35 P.M. on May 14, 1997, surrounded by family and friends. Everyone got to say their final good-byes, and he went very peacefully—he just quit breathing. I had a close friend who stayed with me that night because I really wasn't in any state of mind to be alone, nor did I want to be!

As would be expected, I had a very difficult time falling asleep when everyone finally convinced me that I needed to rest. I was lying on my husband's side of the bed, where Joe breathed his last breath just 12 hours previously. I wasn't asleep, but in that in-between state, where you're still aware of what's going on around you.

I was lying on my side with my hands under the side of my face. I felt Joe touch my arm, and I smelled his particular scent. It was a very brief experience, but nonetheless real. I bolted upright in bed and began to cry copiously. It was what I had wanted so badly, but it came so quickly after his death that I was startled and a bit frightened.

At first I thought I was really "losing it." But then I realized that Joe was just fulfilling his promise to me. It's something I will cherish until the day that I pass on to be with him.

୭୰ଓ୰ଓ

No Other Explanation
by Lisa Gayle Davis Flores

In 1983, I was hitchhiking from Oregon to Washington to go to my grandpa's funeral. I was standing on the shoulder of the freeway when an El Camino car came onto the shoulder at 55 miles per hour. It hit me in the lower back.

I flew through the air and hit the ground. I really thought I was dead, but then I felt somebody put their hands on my shoulders and pick me up. But when I looked to see who had helped me, no one was there. I was also one month pregnant at the time. I believe that this was my guardian angel, saving my unborn child. I will never forget it.

❦❦❦

Eternally Blooming
by Barb Hacking

I recently attended a "Celebration of Life" for Kim, a friend who had passed away after a long illness, leaving behind two young children and a loving husband. One of the speakers at this celebration was her sister, who spoke of how a tulip would now always remind her of Kim. When Kim found out that she probably wouldn't be alive in the spring, she planted lots of tulip bulbs. What a cheerful, loving reminder of her love for her family each spring!

When I returned home that night, I went into my seven-year-old daughter's bedroom to read her a story. Before I started, Rachel leaned over and told me I smelled like tulips. Wow! Children really are so in tune to what is going on around them. She had not been to the celebration, and she had no idea about the legacy of tulips that Kim had left behind.

❦❦❦

Just Ask
by Linda A. Harlow

When I was about 23, I was with a group of people who were discussing the spiritual experiences they'd had. Almost everyone in the group, except for me, had had some sort of spiritual encounter or experience. I had studied and practiced spiritual matters throughout my life, so I wondered why *I* never had any experiences like the special ones that my friends were describing.

One of my friends comforted me by telling me that it was only recently that he'd had a spiritual experience. It happened one evening when he'd pleaded with God with all his heart for just some sign to show that He was there! My friend said aloud to God, "Just something, anything, like the smell of a rose, anything!"At that very instant, he smelled the powerful scent of a rose.

Because this story was so believable to me, I went home and prayed and pleaded that night, and I got myself in a highly emotional state. I also asked for a sign that I was not alone and that I was being heard. Suddenly, a male voice said inside my head, "Don't go any further; you're not ready for it yet." Strangely, this calmed me down, and I assume that this simple response was my answer.

❦❦❦

The Hands of My Angel
by Marianne LoBasso

I was running for the train while it was in motion leaving the station. I ran and jumped onto the train but was twisted around. Still holding on to the handle of the car door, I dropped between the two cars.

My body was between the wheels of the train and the platform. The train was moving, and all I felt were two hands on my back pushing me over the tracks toward the gravel and closer to the platform. But no one was there!

This all happened in a matter of seconds. Even today, I can feel the force of those hands on my back. I know I always have angels following me. No one could believe that I came out of that fall without even a scratch on me!

❧❧❧

An Angel's Kiss
by Maya Tonisson

My romantic partner passed away on June 18, 1999, at the age of 26. He had suffered a hemorrhage in his brain, and after an operation and one week in a coma in intensive care, he let himself go. I was 25, and beside myself, having never experienced losing a partner—or for that matter, anyone in my life who was so young. He was pronounced dead at about 5 or 6 A.M., and I stayed with a friend that night, not wanting to be alone.

The following evening, however, I chose to stay home alone, and after I got into bed, I reached a state of "twilight sleep." I was half awake, half asleep, when I felt my partner lie beside me, and he kissed me very softly. After a few moments, I jolted awake, sat up and opened my eyes, and he was gone. I never saw him, but I still believe to this day that what I felt was real.

❧❧❧

Watched Over by an Angel
by Rosanelia A. Lopez-Leal

Growing up, we had a neighbor whom I'll call "John" who was about eight years older than I was and the same age as my brothers. My mom thought of him as another son. John was the most playful person I've ever met.

I moved away and we all grew up. My brother and his family remained John's parents' neighbors. We all kept in touch with each other, and I finally moved back into town. A few years later, we found out that John was terminally ill. We asked John's mom if we could see him one last time, and she agreed. I had no idea what to expect.

I walked into John's room, and I saw a man lying in bed, unaware of his surroundings. He was not the tall, strong man I'd always remembered. I couldn't stand to see him that way and ran out of the room crying. We finally left John's house. I knew that the end was near for our friend.

That night, something woke me up at 2:55 A.M. I was lying on my side, facing the wall. I could feel someone's penetrating eyes peering at me. When I opened my eyes, I sensed the being moving to my bedroom door. My kitten stared at the door with a frightened looked on her face. I was scared of what I would see, but I knew that it was John, and I knew that he had just passed on. I figured that he wanted to say good-bye to me since I couldn't do so earlier that afternoon.

I started talking to John, and I told him that I wouldn't be afraid of him and that I would help his parents and new family. It was the most peaceful experience I had ever felt. I knew it was John, and I knew he had passed away. I figured that he wanted to comfort me since I broke down by his bed earlier that day. After I confirmed my peacefulness with him, I felt that he left the room.

At about 9 A.M., my brother called me to say that John had indeed passed away. I told him, "I know." There was silence from my brother. I didn't cry because I just knew that John was in a better place. It took a few months before I shared this story with his parents. They believed me and agreed that it was their son.

A couple of years after John's death, my husband had to keep late hours with his university studies. This meant that I would stay at home alone until the early hours of the morning. I would try to stay up to wait for my husband, but I got too tired and would go to bed.

I would always feel someone touching my leg with both hands. I could feel that slight pressure of the fingers. After several nights of this, I made up my mind that it was John being my guardian angel and telling me that he was with me and that I shouldn't be scared. I looked forward to this every time my husband would be late coming home. I was not scared as long as I felt my friend's presence.

My husband finally finished that project and doesn't need to stay out late anymore. Consequently, I no longer feel John's presence. I'm glad that my friend became my guardian angel during that semester. Every once in a while, I feel his presence near me. Because of John, I know that angels do exist. I feel that God sent John as my angel to help me through those nights when I was alone.

❦❦❦

Bubble of Protection
by Mary Weirick

When I was 13 years old, I went to a Little League baseball game to meet some friends who were cheerleaders. After the game, I looked for my friends so I could get a ride home, but they had already left. In fact, everyone I knew had left. It was late, and my house was more than a mile away.

I had been warned never to be out after dark alone, and I was terrified. I started to cry as I walked home through the dimly lit neighborhood. I had gone about a block when an inner voice told me to ask for help. So I prayed that God would protect me. Immediately, I felt myself enclosed in a beautiful blue bubble. I knew that I was safe, loved, and cared for. I walked the rest of the way home without fear, knowing I was safe.

I remember the joy, wonder, and trust I felt at that time. I'm very grateful to my angels for their love, protection, and guidance.

₯ ₯ ₯

PART II

*True Stories of People
Who Have Seen Angels**

CHAPTER FIFTEEN

Opening to Heaven

W e all have angel encounters continually, but many of us aren't aware of these occurrences. They can be subtle, that's for sure. So, in this section, we'll explore how to bring your heavenly connections to the level of conscious awareness. When you're aware of the presence of your angels and deceased loved ones, you'll enjoy them, and benefit from them more.

If you want to make contact with your angels, deceased loved ones, or an ascended master, these next few chapters will describe some methods that can help you. These are the same techniques that I teach my psychic-development students, and they're also the same ones that I use myself before I give readings. They're very powerful.

Most people feel some ambivalence about contacting heavenly beings. On the one hand, they desperately want to see an angel or departed loved one. But they also fear seeing a frightening image. "Will I be opening myself up to seeing dark beings? Or will my deceased loved one look ghoulish?" These are natural concerns, as people worry about losing control, or being frightened out of their wits.

So, one of my wishes is that the stories I related in *Angel Visions* and continue to chronicle here in *Angel Visions II* will boost your confidence that heavenly encounters are positive, happy experiences. Know that you won't see upsetting images when your angels and deceased loved ones pay you a visit.

While it's true that there are "unsavory" beings in heaven, they are a slim minority compared to all the magnificent angels and guides constantly swimming around us on the etheric plane.

One of the greatest angels of all, Archangel Michael, can prevent you from having a frightening encounter. All you need to do is mentally say to him:

> *"Archangel Michael, please escort away from me anyone who is not my angel, guide, or a being who expresses God's Divine light."*

Michael needs to receive this sort of explicit request because God's Law of Free Will prevents him from helping us unless we ask.

Archangel Michael is able to be with everyone simultaneously who calls upon him, and there are no time or space restraints. So it's a good idea to ask Archangel Michael to stay permanently stationed by your side. Ask him to screen the beings in your life—both the physical and the spiritual ones—so that only benevolent beings surround you. Once you've asked Michael for help, you can relax. This request is always granted for everyone, regardless of lifestyle, religion, or character. So don't worry that your requests might be denied. They can't be!

It's important to clear fears out of the way because they can prevent you from having a heavenly encounter. Ambivalent people are putting one foot on the gas pedal and one on the brakes simultaneously, which keeps them from moving forward.

Trying Too Hard

Another issue that prevents people from seeing their angels and deceased loved ones is the fear of failure. This fear often makes people push and strain to have an angel encounter. They try to force it to happen, which blocks the experience completely. The sad irony is that the people who love angels the most are often the ones who have the hardest time seeing them!

Almost every weekend at my workshops, I see the following scenario played out: An angel-loving woman will arrive, dressed in an angel sweatshirt, angel earrings, and an angel necklace. She'll be accompanied by her loving husband, who really couldn't care less about angels, but is just coming to the workshop to please his wife.

Then the workshop begins, and before lunchtime, I've guided the audience through an exercise that helps them see angels. The husband is seeing angels and deceased loved ones, and he says to his wife, "Wow, honey, this is amazing! Thanks for bringing me to this conference." She, meanwhile, has had no success at seeing angels, and snaps, "How come *you're* seeing angels? You don't even like them!"

Her frustration stems from her underlying belief that since she's a member of the angel "fan club," she's entitled to insider privileges. But the angels are equally devoted to all of us, even to nonbelievers and newcomers. Her main block has to do with the fact that she desperately wants to see angels, so she's trying too hard to make it happen. Her husband, who has a nonchalant attitude about heaven, is relaxed and more open to the experience. One such husband recently completed my Angel Therapy Practitioner certification course, and he's now a professional angel reader. Yet he was originally a "drag-along" at one of my workshops a couple of years ago.

So, straining and pushing can actually prevent us from connecting with our angels. The fear that causes us to force things to happen comes from feeling alone, and the belief that "if it's going to be, it's up to me." However, our angel encounters are derived from the power of God, the angels, ascended masters, and our deceased loved ones. A teamwork approach to angel encounters works best.

Clearing the Fear

In addition to calling upon Archangel Michael's presence, here are two other ways to diminish or eliminate fear blocks:

1. Freezer method. Write your fears on a piece of paper. You can either write an elaborate description of your fears, or just a general "fear of being psychic" sentence. Then, put the paper into your refrigerator's freezer compartment. If you live with skeptics, it's best to put the paper in the back of the freezer, where it will be unnoticed, or freeze it in a small container of water. Leave the paper in the freezer for a minimum of three months. This method also works well with anything in your life that you'd like to release, including problems with relationships, addictions, or money issues.

2. Dream method. The angels do some of their best work while we're sleeping. Why? Because our fears are asleep at that time, so we're more open to angelic assistance. Before you go to sleep at night, mentally ask Archangel Michael, Archangel Raphael (who's in charge of physical healings), and Archangel Uriel (whose area is emotional and psychological healings) to enter your dreams. Mentally say to them:

"Please enter my dream, my body, my mind, and my heart, and clear away any fears or unforgiveness that could be blocking me from having a conscious angel encounter."

Intention Is Everything

The angels have a phrase that they love to repeat: "Your intentions create your experiences." This means that our underlying expectations steer us toward the type of experiences we have as a result. If we hold positive expectations about our angel encounters, we'll have positive results.

However, if we have negative intentions, such as, "Gee, I sure hope I can do this," or "I'm afraid to see the spirit world," or "Will God punish me for doing this?" then we will be blocked from having an angel encounter. For one thing, the angels love us deeply, and they wouldn't do anything to frighten us, such as showing up if we don't really want to see them. The same goes for your deceased loved ones. Your grandparents, Mom, Dad, siblings, or other loved ones see your fear as a giant "Keep Away!" sign. They will respect that boundary out of love.

"I really want to see my mom, but I'm afraid that she'll have Aunt Edna with her. And I don't want any contact with Aunt Edna!" said Betsy, a woman at one of my seminars. She explained that her aunt had been bossy and verbally abusive. Betsy was afraid that by seeing her mother, she'd be opening the gates of heaven so that other "less desirable" relatives would show up uninvited. This is another area to delegate to Archangel Michael, who's happy to act as your "bouncer" angel. He'll direct traffic, if you just ask him to.

One of the reasons why children are so psychic is because

of their positive intentions. They don't worry, "Am I making this up, or is it real?" Children know that reality comes in many flavors. They also trust their intuition to a higher degree than most adults. Additionally, their lives are simpler than adults, in general, so their minds are less cluttered with distractions, worries, pressure, and noise.

So, to open yourself to an encounter with heaven, be "as a little child." Let go of rigid expectations about your angel connection. Just hold a positive intention such as, "I'd really like to meet my guardian angel," or "I would love to see and talk with Mom," and then release the desire to the winds of the Universe. Trust your angels to catch your wish and bring it to you in a delightfully surprising way.

That's why it's important not to dictate to God how you want your angel encounter to be. For instance, don't say to the angels, "Please brush my hair as a sign that you're with me." Instead, simply say, "Please give me a sign that you're with me," and let them figure out the best method for delivering that request. Remind yourself frequently that the "how" of the way prayers are answered is up to God, not up to us. The infinite creativity of the Divine Mind is filled with happy surprises that defy the physical laws of Earth, which our human mind often worries about.

So, holding positive intentions is essential. Even if you don't fully believe in angel encounters because you haven't yet experienced one firsthand, hold a positive intention. Even if you're not sure if you're qualified or deserving of an angel encounter (I assure you that you are!), hold a positive intention. Even if you want to see an angel or deceased loved one so badly that it hurts, hold a positive intention.

Here are some affirmations to help you elevate your intentions to the most positive and optimistic level possible. Read, write, or say these affirmations as often as possible:

- *I feel safe opening up my psychic abilities.*

- *I am highly visual.*

- *I am very clairvoyant.*

- *I easily hear the voice of God and the angels.*

- *I am open to seeing my deceased loved ones.*

- *I welcome my angels into my dreams.*

- *God and the angels love me very much.*

- *I can feel the presence of angels around me right now.*

- *God and the angels speak to me continually.*

- *I notice signs from heaven.*

- *I am open to Divine communication.*

- *I trust God to protect me.*

Answered Prayers

The Law of Free Will says that heaven cannot intervene or interfere in our lives unless we give it permission. The only exception is to save our lives—if it isn't our time yet to go. So, you'll need to request that your angels help you to clearly see, hear, or feel their presence. There are many ways to do so, including the following:

Praying. State your request to God and the angels. For example, "God, I deeply desire to meet my guardian angel. Please help me see and hear this angel." Say this prayer repeatedly until you feel a sense of peace and inevitability in your heart and gut area.

Directly asking. Many people encounter a deceased loved one directly after asking that person for help. You can do so aloud, in written form, or silently. Let's say that you're worried about a particular deceased loved one. Ask that person for some sort of reassurance that everything is okay. That person will then contact you, either through a dream visitation, an apparition encounter, or by giving you a sign. If your experience isn't clear enough for you, then ask the person for additional contact.

Writing a letter. This technique works best when conducted in an isolated environment. So, go find a quiet place outdoors, or squirrel away in your corner of the house (including the bathroom, if there's no other private place!). Write a letter to God, your guardian angels, or your deceased loved one. Pour out your heart about your desire for an angel encounter, and your fears or reservations. End the letter with a strong request for their help.

Using possessions. Kirlian photography shows that an object's aura is affected by the emotions of the person who held it. In other words, the energy of a person is imprinted upon their possessions. As such, you can tune in to your deceased loved one by holding one of their possessions in the hand you normally don't write with (that is, your energy-receiving hand). It's best to hold an object that your loved one came into constant contact with—for instance, a ring, watch, eyeglasses, or a necklace. Metal objects hold the energy best, but any possession will do in a pinch. You can also hold a person's photograph as a way of tuning in to their energy.

As you hold the object, close your eyes and hold the intention of psychically connecting with that person. Ask your angels to act as telephone operators, routing your call.

Whether you feel your loved one's presence or not, mentally ask the person to contact you.

Going outside in nature. Perhaps the reason why so many people have encounters with their deceased loved ones at gravesites is because they're outdoors. The person's soul certainly doesn't hang around where their bones are buried or their ashes are contained. After death, we no longer identify with our physical bodies! However, when you visit a deceased loved one's grave, you're thinking about them strongly, and you're outside in nature. You can replicate those same two conditions (without visiting the grave) in order to contact your deceased loved one. Simply go to a beautiful place in nature, and hold strong thoughts about your loved one.

This works especially well if you go to a place that reminds you of the departed. For instance, if your deceased loved one was fanatical about the mountains, you might connect more deeply after you hike partway up one. Or, if the two of you loved strolling around the local lake, visit this location and hold the intention of contacting your departed one. As you walk lakeside, imagine that your loved one is beside you, and hold a mental conversation. Before long, you'll probably realize that your loved one *is* there and that your conversation is real!

Holding a ceremony. Just because your loved one's body is gone doesn't mean that you can't celebrate their birthday or other significant date. After my Grandma Pearl passed away, I held a birthday "party" in her honor, complete with a huge bouquet of her favorite flowers (gladiolas) gracing the table. She definitely attended, enjoyed, and appreciated this ceremony from the spirit world.

Your departed family members attend every significant ceremony and get-together that you hold, so don't ignore them! Mentally or verbally say hello to your deceased loved ones whenever you hold a family get-together. They will appreciate being recognized and remembered, and you're more likely to see, hear, or feel their presence.

You can also hold a ceremony in order to contact your guardian angels or ascended masters. For instance, on holidays in Jesus' honor, you might feel especially open and close to him, which could spark an encounter. Or you can create a ceremony to contact your angels and guides, using free-form dance or drumming.

With positive optimism, you will be more open to the angel experiences that are occurring around you continually. Just be open and aware. Your angel connection will most likely happen when you least expect it, since that's when you're most relaxed and open. As discussed here, heavenly encounters can take a variety of forms. Apparition experiences, dream visitations, disembodied voices, encounters with a mysterious stranger, or other signs are just a few of the ways that heaven will answer your prayers.

)€)€)€

CHAPTER SIXTEEN

Seeing: Keys to Clairvoyance

Y ou can connect with heaven through your visions, dreams, thoughts, feelings, or by hearing words. Yet, I find that most people strongly desire to have a *visual* experience with heaven. Perhaps it's because "seeing is believing," but most of my audience members tell me that they'd rather see than hear an angel. And yet, as much as they desire this, they also fear it.

Countless Hollywood movies have taught us that deceased people are only slightly prettier than monsters. According to these films, the deceased look just like they did when they died—gruesome. They have shredded clothing, bandages around their head, and circles beneath their eyes!

Fortunately, Hollywood's imagery of the dead is based on fear, not reality. Probably one of the most accurate movies in portraying the appearance of deceased people is the film *Always*, starring Richard Dreyfuss and Holly Hunter. This movie shows that the deceased look and act like normal, everyday folks, so you can release any fears about seeing blood or gore associated with your deceased loved one.

In this chapter, we'll explore ways to open yourself up to a visual encounter with heaven. As always, you'll find that plenty of angelic assistance is available, provided you ask for the angels' help.

The Angels of Clairvoyance

A powerful group of angels will help you uncover your "third eye," which is the conduit of clairvoyance. These diminutive angels gather around your third eye to cleanse and heal it of psychic debris and imbalances. When I call upon these angels, I can feel them working on my brow and third eye area.

To call them, simply hold the mental thought:

"Angels of Clairvoyance, I call upon you now. Please come to my third eye and clear away any blockages and heal any pain that could block my spiritual sight. Please help me see across the veil. Thank you."

Spend a few moments relaxing with deep breath. Notice any sensations or mental images. Keep your heart open, and be sure to thank the Angels of Clairvoyance after a few moments, even if you're unaware or unsure of their presence.

Then, mentally call upon Archangel Raphael by saying something like, "Archangel Raphael, please come to me now." Imagine for a moment, if you could see Raphael, what he might look like. Visualize or feel Raphael putting his index finger upon your third eye. Be sure to breathe during this process in order to fully accept Raphael's help. He will send healing green light through his finger into your third eye. You may feel heat or pressure between your two eyes. If it becomes painful, mentally ask Raphael to heal the unpleasant sensation.

The Angels of Clairvoyance and Archangel Raphael are available to help you become more clairvoyant. Of course, we need to work in partnership with the angels to achieve any aim. Remember the section on Positive Intention in the previous chapter? Nowhere is that more crucial than when developing clairvoyance. Doubts draw a dark curtain across the third eye, and optimism opens the window of clear vision.

"I Am Highly Visual"

In the previous chapter, we discussed using affirmations to inspire an angelic encounter. In a similar vein, it's important to avoid using negative affirmations about your clairvoyant abilities. So many of my psychic-development students complain to me that they're "just not visual." They describe themselves as being unable to see anything when they close their eyes.

Yet, scientific studies show that everyone has visual dreams, whether they consciously remember them or not. It's impossible to *not* be visual. Granted, some people are wired to be primarily visual in their orientation. They notice how every thing and everyone looks, instead of how their environment sounds or feels. Yet, every single person picks up on visual cues, even the blind!

If you tell yourself that you aren't visual, then your unconscious mind reads this like a command. I tell students, "I can't help you if you've decided you're not visual." So, I always emphasize the need to positively affirm what we desire, even if it feels false or fake in the beginning. Eventually, reality always catches up to our affirmations and mirrors what we're claiming. In other words, if you affirm, "I am highly visual," your unconscious mind will deliver that reality to you. You'll not only develop the ability to see the spirit world, but you'll also be able to hold mental images of reading material, and the faces of new acquaintances, in your mind's eye. Being highly visual is quite handy!

Crystal and Energy Work on the Third Eye

During my longer psychic-development courses, I perform crystal and energy work on my students' third eye. This method has been quite powerful in opening stubborn third eyes. You can conduct it on yourself, but it's probably more effective to have an empathetic person (especially a trained energy healer) conduct this session:

Put the index and middle fingers of your right hand on top of the third eye. Place the same fingers of your left hand on the back of the head. Visualize a bright beam of white light jumping from your right to your left hand. This beam of light clears out obstructions within the head and third eye. You'll receive information about the nature of the third-eye blockage, which can also help. For instance, you might be told about a particular past incident that made the person fear spiritual visions. This method also works well if you hold a piece of clear quartz crystal in your right hand.

Removing the Eye Covering

This method needs a second person to conduct the healing work. Whenever a painful or frightening incident occurs, related to our clairvoyance, we build a wall around our third eye. This is similar to putting a wall around your heart to protect yourself from repeated emotional hurt.

The painful incidents related to blocked clairvoyance largely stem from childhood incidents. Here are common childhood experiences that can cause someone to shut down their third eye:

- *Scoldings.* A clairvoyant child is punished or lectured for being spiritually gifted. The child is told that this is evil or crazy, or is accused of lying.

- *Frights.* Having a negative vision about a future event that comes true, and thinking that you, the child, somehow caused or could have prevented the occurrence. Seeing frightening images or beings.

- *Teasing.* Being told that you're weird or too sensitive, or feeling like you don't belong or fit in because of your spiritual sight.

- *Invalidation.* Being told that what you're seeing or hearing isn't real. "Your invisible friend doesn't really exist, and you need to grow up."

- *Judgments.* Being called a "know-it-all," which is based in truth, since the child is tapped in to the collective knowledge of the Divine Mind.

Most people who are blocked because of childhood incidents remember having visual experiences in their youth. People who claim that they've never experienced any clairvoyance often went through painful incidents prior to their childhood. In other words, their blocks stem from past lives. Whether you believe in past lives or not, the healing method I'll soon describe is very effective and shouldn't be skipped just because of philosophical differences.

Here are some of the past-life incidents that commonly create third-eye blockages:

Death or torture. Countless metaphysicians and spiritual seekers were killed during the Spanish Inquisition and Salem witch hunts. Death was brutal, often by burning or hanging the spiritually gifted individual.

Ridicule. Some people were put into stocks in the middle of town and had stones or other objects pelted at them.

Loss. Some even had their children or property taken away from them.

Witnessing traumatic events. Being present at an overwhelmingly violent event, such as a war or the crucifixion, has caused some people to shut down, because they never want to *see* again.

Those who have experienced painful incidents in their childhood or past lives (related to clairvoyance), often form a covering over their third eye to shield themselves. The shield is like a bandage, covering old wounds.

To remove the covering, you'll need to work with another person. Preferably, this other person is empathetic and intuitive. Trying this method with a judgmental person or a skeptic could cause you to further shrink away from clairvoyance.

Here are the steps:

1. Hold your hand one-half inch from the person's third eye.

2. Pretend you're going to pull off a large, circular adhesive bandage that's covering the third-eye area.

3. Pull the bandage off fast, just like you would when pulling one off a child's wound.

4. Immediately place the middle finger of your "writing hand" on top of the person's third eye.

5. See or feel yourself sending healing energy to the person's third eye.

6. Simultaneously, have a mental talk with the third eye. Ask it, "What is hurting you? What has frightened you?"

7. Listen, with your intuition, thoughts, vision, and inner ear, to the third eye's answer. Like a patient at a doctor's office, the third eye will tell you its story about why it has hidden itself away.

8. Relay this information to the other person while you continue to heal and reassure the third eye with your loving energy.

9. If you need to, help the other person to release old anger, fears, or unforgiveness. Encourage the person to say, *"I am willing to release this situation and all accompanying hurt to God and the angels. I ask that the effects of the situation be undone in all directions of time, and that all karma be balanced for everyone concerned."*

Clairvoyant Experiences

There are numerous types of clairvoyant experiences. Having a clairvoyant experience involves:

- *asking* for the experience, or praying for help;

- *noticing* the answer that comes as something that you see;

- *trusting* what you see; and

- *following through* on any guidance that comes from your clairvoyant vision.

Signs from Above

The first type of clairvoyant experience involves seeing signs. Some people write these experiences off as coincidence so they never notice that their prayers are answered.

Here are some common ways in which heaven gives us validation and guidance through the use of signs. If you see or experience any of these occurrences three or more times, please pay attention, because you're getting a sign from above. Most of the time, signs are simply a way for heaven to say, "Hello, I'm here with you!" But if you suspect that your angel or loved one has more to say, be sure to ask for clarification. Just mentally say, "I really want to know what you're trying to tell me, but I'm not clear what this sign means. Please give me additional clarification." If you want to know who in heaven has sent you this sign, you can also ask to receive this information.

Common Types of Signs

- *Angel lights.* Seeing sparkling lights, or a flash of light that reminds you of a camera's flashbulb. "Angel lights" result from the friction of your angels moving across time and space.

- *Animals' reactions.* Your dog barks at the wall as if he's seeing someone there. Your cat suddenly streaks out of the room because of something she's seen.

- *Butterflies, birds, and moths.* Seeing dozens of these flying beings, or one particular one that looks at you or follows you.

- *Clouds.* Seeing an angel-shaped cloud as a reminder that your loved one is in heaven with the angels, and that the angels are watching over you.

- *Coins.* Finding "pennies from heaven" in odd locations.

- *Feathers.* Finding a feather in an odd location, or seeing a feather float from the sky toward you.

- *Flowers.* Seeing flowers that were your loved one's favorite, or *your* favorite.

- *Interrupted television reception or flickering lights.* The television blinks on suddenly, reception is interrupted momentarily, or the lights dim or flicker.

- *Moved objects.* You *know* that you put your necklace in the jewelry case, but now it's on the shelf.

- *Number sequences.* Every time you look at the clock or a license plate, it says "111," or some other repeated number sequence. (My book *Healing with the Angels* [Hay House, 1999], provides the meaning behind these number sequences.)

- *Rainbows.* You see a rainbow in the sky, and you intuitively know it's a sign from a deceased loved one that everything is okay. Or, you repeatedly see rainbow designs, decals, and insignias in unexpected locations.

- *Word and phrase repetition.* Every time you look at a newspaper, magazine, or friends' e-mails, you read the same words or phrases. For instance, I kept receiving unsolicited articles about swimming with dolphins until I finally complied.

Corner-of-the-Eye Visions

Another type of clairvoyant experience involves visions that you see peripherally. For example, you see a person out of the corner of your eye, but when you turn to look, the person is gone. The periphery (or corner) of our eyes are more sensitive to movement and light than the front of our eyes, so you probably really are seeing angels and guides out of the corner of your eye. But when you turn to look straight ahead, you lose the eye's sensitivities.

As you're looking into the bathroom mirror, you see a person standing behind you. You turn around quickly, but no one is there. Very often, we see fleeting images of people when our eyes are relaxed, such as when we're shaving or putting on makeup and looking into the bathroom mirror.

Mental Images

Still another form of clairvoyance happens when you see a picture or movie in your mind's eye. You meet a new person and see a mental movie of them screaming and yelling. Although you've only just met, and they're smiling and pleasant, you know from the vision that they possess a hot temper.

For example, my mother was upset because her next-door neighbor's air conditioning unit was extremely loud. It whirred, buzzed, and shrieked loudly, interrupting my mother's peace and quiet. She prayed for help and received a mental movie of a white air conditioning repair van parked in her neighbor's driveway. A few hours later, the scene came true, and her neighbor's air conditioner was fixed and quieted.

Meditation Visions and Invocations

Several of the angel-encounter stories included in *Angel Visions* and *Angel Visions II* happened when the person was meditating. You can have a very real encounter with a heavenly being by meditating in a quiet location. Hold the intention of meeting someone in heaven, or ask a question and allow heaven to "assign" an angel, deceased loved one, or ascended master to answer your query.

Close your eyes, breathe deeply, and keep an open mind. You might see a detailed vision of the being, or have an experience similar to a waking dream, where you travel and interact with other beings. Or, your meditation might be more vague, where you encounter shapes or lights. Any form of meditation has powerfully healing effects and is a worthwhile endeavor.

Dream Visitations

Scientists at the University of Virginia have studied dream visitations, where a person dreams about a deceased loved one. Drs. Ian Stevenson and John Palmer have concluded that "vividness" is the indicator that the experience is a true visitation and not just a dream. Vividness means that the colors in the dream are intense, the emotions are strong, the message imparted is clear, and the memory of the dream doesn't fade afterward.

You can invoke a dream visitation for yourself, or it can happen spontaneously in response to your prayers or worries. The majority of dream visitations are comforting and healing. Occasionally, though, a person will dream about a loved one who delivers a cryptic message. The person wakes up wondering, *What did that mean?* As with koan riddles, the answer may only come intuitively, with no concrete confirmation.

To invoke a dream visitation, first hold a mental conversation with, or write a letter to, a particular deceased loved one, your guardian angel, or an ascended master. Request that this being enter your dreams, but don't specify when this will occur. If you need reassurance or guidance about an issue, be sure to request this help.

Eat lightly, and avoid mind- or mood-altering drugs or alcohol, which can interfere with dream transmissions. Exercise early in the day to ensure a good night's sleep. Take a warm bath or shower before going to bed to relax you further. Make sure that your sleeping conditions are comfortable, with fresh sheets and a quiet, dark room.

Before falling asleep at night, reiterate your intention and desire to connect. Mentally ask the being to enter your dreams. Also, ask Archangel Michael to help you with your desire for a dream visitation. It's important not to strain, push, or try to force a dream visitation to occur. Also, don't allow yourself to become frustrated if the dream is delayed, don't get angry with the deceased loved one if they don't show up immediately, and don't get jealous of another person who's had a dream visitation. Anger and judgments come from our ego, and our ego isn't psychic. Pray for angelic assistance if you go into your ego during your dream invocations.

If you hold the intention, ask for help, and stay open, your desire for a dream visitation will likely occur within a few days. The dream will seem more-than-real, and you will know that it wasn't just a mere dream. You really did visit with a being from the other side!

Many dream visitations have healing results. For instance, one of my workshop members told me that she and her father had never gotten along very well. They had argued throughout his life, and he died without either one making amends. She prayed for a way to heal this situation. Several days later, she had this dream:

"I was sitting on top of a large hill with my father. He had been a hat maker, and he was wearing one of his favorite black felt hats. I could see many people at the bottom of the hill who seemed to be standing and staring at us, although they were too far away for me to recognize any faces. Mostly, I was focused on my father. We healed so many of our misunderstandings, and we told each other 'I love you,' and we hugged.

*"When I woke up from the dream, I knew that
something had deeply healed between me and my
father. That afternoon at lunch, I told a friend
of mine, who had never met my father, about the
dream. Before I could finish describing the dream,
she gasped and said, 'Oh! I just remembered that I
dreamt about you last night! I was at the bottom of a
hill, and I saw you and a man with a black hat sitting on the top of the hill talking. I couldn't see the
details of your faces, but I knew it was you, and I
saw the two of you hug.'"*

Apparition Experiences

Every person whom I've ever interviewed about an apparition experience reports the same thing: It is an extremely
pleasurable encounter, with no fear. The living person knows
that it isn't a dream. Typically, a person wakes up in the middle of the night and sees a bluish-white glow at the foot of their
bed. They see the diminutive figure of a deceased loved one.
Wordlessly, they exchange communication through mind-to-
mind telepathy. The departed one says, "I'm fine. Don't worry
about me. Please go on with your life. I love you," and then may
offer some heartfelt guidance. Afterward, the living person
feels relieved and healed of grieving. That makes sense, because
much of the grieving process stems from the following:

- *Missing the person.* The encounter is exactly
  like being with the person in the flesh. Many
  people report that they smell and feel the touch
  of their loved one during the visit.

- ***Worrying about the person.*** The deceased loved one alleviates concerns, and assures the living person, "I'm okay."

- ***Anger.*** The apparition experience heals misunderstandings. For instance, you might worry that your deceased loved one is angry because you didn't visit enough, or weren't at the deathbed. I've actually never met a deceased loved one who was angry about these issues! Nonetheless, it's comforting to hear forgiveness expressed, or to impart forgiveness in a face-to-face meeting.

You can invoke an apparition experience simply by asking for one. Keep in mind, however, that the average apparition visit lasts only five minutes, and most people only have one such visit with a deceased loved one. It takes a tremendous amount of energy for a departed one to appear in apparition form. Sometimes they must "borrow" energy from their own guides in order to make a visit. It's easier for them to enter our dreams than to appear as a waking apparition.

I've interviewed many families in which only one family member saw an apparition of a departed relative. The other family members wondered, *Maybe the departed loved one doesn't love me as much as the person who had the apparition experience.* But the factors that determine who in the family will have an apparition experience are more subjective than being "most lovable." It isn't a popularity contest.

It seems that those family members who are most relaxed have the greatest number of apparition experiences. Other factors include being sober. So many times, grief-stricken people turn to alcohol or other drugs (illicit and prescription) to ease their pain. These drugs actually block them from having an apparition experience that could heal their pain!

I've also found that those who appeal to the deceased person with pleas of help often have apparition experiences as a result. "Please, Grandma, I need to know that you're okay!" may precipitate Grandma's appearance in your bedroom so that she can personally reassure you.

In Summary

Clairvoyance takes many forms, and it's important to appreciate and trust any visual communication that you receive from heaven. I also recommend keeping a journal of your clairvoyant experiences, since record-keeping seems to trigger (or, at least, increase the awareness of) psychic experiences.

Our angel encounters can also involve hearing a voice, a noise, or a phrase. Clairaudience (or clear hearing) can be developed in the same manner as clairvoyance, as you'll read about in the next chapter.

𝈁 𝈁 𝈁

CHAPTER SEVENTEEN

Hearing: Keys to Clairaudience

W hen I was a student in an undergraduate psychology program, our teachers told us that hearing a voice was a sign of insanity. Little did I know at the time that I'd someday be teaching people to hear the voice of Spirit. The truth that I now know is that hearing the voice of God is the sanest thing that we can experience.

The loud, direct voices that you read about in Chapter 10 are usually reserved for emergency situations. Most of the time, God and the angels speak to us in softer, gentler tones. This requires us to turn down the volume in our mind and our surroundings.

However, heaven also does try to help us hear them clearly. My mother had a situation that I've seen in several other people since. She really wanted to hear the voice of heaven, so she mentally said to her guides during meditation, "A little louder, please."

Still, she heard nothing. But she could feel the presence of beings close to her, and she sensed that they were trying to say something to her. "Louder, please!" my mother prayed.

After pleading for an increase in their heavenly volume, she suddenly heard her grandmother's voice saying, "I'm right here!" in a piercingly loud tone.

God, the angels, and our guides welcome our feedback during our conversations. If you cannot hear or understand them, please speak up! Ask them to talk louder, and to explain cryptic remarks to you.

I'm often asked, "How do I know the difference between true angelic communication and my own imagination?" There are several key distinguishing characteristics to notice:

__True Angelic Guidance__	__False Guidance__
Loving and warm	Negative and abusive
Supportive	Discouraging
Brief and to the point	Overly verbal
Begins sentences with the words *You* or *We*	Begins sentences with the word *I*
Talks about how you can help others	Talks about how you can get something from others
Encourages you to pursue your dreams	Doubts whether your dreams can come true
Inspires you to develop your talents	Distracts you from applying your talents
Asks you to balance your time usage	Guides you to overfocus on one life area

Forms of Clairaudient Contact

As you've read in the stories in this book, clairaudient angel encounters take many forms. Some people hear lifesaving warnings. Other people hear messages in answer to their prayers. For instance, a woman named Mary told me that she was unhappy being a nurse at a large health organization. She prayed for guidance, and within days, she heard a loud male voice say, *Pick up your purse and go to Wal-Mart.* Mary was dismayed. She didn't want to work at Wal-Mart; she wanted to stay in nursing! The voice repeated itself: *Pick up your purse and go to Wal-Mart.* "But I don't need anything at the store," she argued. *Pick up your purse and go to Wal-Mart, now!* The voice commanded. What would *you* have done?

Mary picked up her purse and drove to Wal-Mart. She felt as if she was in a *Twilight Zone* episode as she drove. Why was she going? What would she do when she got there?

As she pulled into the Wal-Mart parking lot, another car was pulling out of the same driveway. Mary did a double-take, because she recognized the two women in the other car. It was Susan and Barbara from nursing school! Quickly rolling down her window, Mary blurted out, "Do you have a job for me?" Susan and Barbara smiled in recognition of Mary, and said, "Yes, as a matter of fact, we do." They were helping to open a small clinic and were searching for another nurse for the clinic's staff. Mary now works at that clinic, and she's so happy that she *picked up her purse and went to Wal-Mart!*

Wouldn't it be nice if all our Divine guidance was delivered so clearly? Most people, under daily circumstances, hear softer and more subtle guidance. Sometimes the auditory guidance is even cryptic. Here are some of the more common ways in which we experience clairaudience:

- *Hearing your name called.* As you're waking up in the morning, you hear a disembodied voice saying your name. You wonder who it is and what the experience means. (Usually, it's just a relative saying "Hi" to you. They can get through easier when you're still in the alpha brain wave state of lucid dreaming, immediately before you wake up.)

- *Hearing disembodied music.* A strain of gorgeous celestial music wafts for a brief moment, from a location outside of your head, but not attached to any physical source of music. This often comes from your higher consciousness making a connection with the astral plane during soul travels in your sleep. You're hearing "the music of the spheres," or heaven. People who have had near-death experiences report that they hear the most unearthly, beautiful music in the afterlife plane.

- *Ringing in one ear.* A high-pitched ringing that occurs from out-of-the-blue in one ear (usually the right one). Most of the people who experience this phenomenon are lightworkers. This is a tone that has two main purposes: It's a compressed file of information that's downloaded to lightworkers to help them on their missions; it's a frequency that elevates the consciousness and energy level of the lightworker. If the ringing is uncomfortably loud, you can ask your angels to turn down the volume.

- *Hearing a song in your head.* In the case of deceased loved ones, they often say hello by sending you a signal through their favorite song. You can make a repetitious song stop by saying hello to your deceased loved one, and asking that person to stop transmitting the song's signal to you.

- *Hearing a song on the radio repeatedly.* If you continually hear your loved one's (deceased or living) favorite song on the radio, it probably means that they're thinking about you. If you hear a song repeatedly that doesn't have a relationship tie, then listen closely to its lyrics, because your angels may be using the song to convey a message to you. When I was considering writing the book *Constant Craving*, I suddenly heard the k.d. lang song of the same name played constantly, even though the song was no longer a current hit. I told my editor, Jill Kramer, about this experience, and we both agreed that it was a sign to produce the book, which we did.

• ***Overhearing a conversation.*** You're trying to make an important decision, and you pray for guidance. An hour later, you happen to overhear a snippet of conversation that has a bearing on your situation. Did you just "happen" to hear this message, or did your angels make sure that you heard it? I believe it's the latter.

• ***A message from TV or radio.*** My friend Jonathan Robinson (author of *The Experience of God*, Hay House, 1994) felt drawn to travel to India to meet the avatar Sai Baba, but he worried whether it was the right time to go. After all, it was a very long, expensive, and time-consuming journey. He prayed for guidance, and when he came home, something made him turn on his television set. Just then, a television preacher looked at his congregation and said, "You need to go to India!" That was enough of a sign for Jonathan, who ended up having a life-changing meeting with Sai Baba.

Another example is a Phoenix woman who just happened to turn on her radio while driving to her doctor's office to have a lump in her breast biopsied. She heard me being interviewed about angels on the *Beth and Bill Show* just as I was saying, "We must ask our angels for help before they're allowed to intervene."

Of course! the woman said to herself. *I forgot to ask my angels to help me!* While driving, she appealed to her angels for healing and help. At her appointment, the doctor was unable to find the lump. It had disappeared, and the woman credits her angels. She's quite happy that she followed her guidance to turn on the radio that morning.

- *Hearing an inner voice.* A soft inner voice gives you guidance or a loving warning. You know that it's true angelic guidance if there's a quality that someone else is speaking to you with love and encouragement. It may even sound like your own voice. True guidance is also repetitive, so you're likely to hear the same voice or thought repeatedly until you heed its advice.

- *Hearing a warning.* A crisp, clear, and disembodied voice ushers a loving command of action. You almost feel hypnotized into obeying, as if angels have anesthetized you. Later, you realize that the voice saved you from injury, death, or other forms of loss.

- *A mysterious stranger's comforting message.* You're worried about something and pray for angelic assistance. Later that day, a complete stranger approaches you and offers unsolicited, comforting words. You feel much better afterward, but wonder who that person was and how they knew about your situation.

- *A loved one's comforting message.* A friend or family member utters just the phrase that you need to hear, without that person being aware of it. That person is unknowingly channeling your angel, like a telephone call from God.

- *An angel or deceased loved one's whisper or voice.* When I'm giving angel readings, I'll hear my client's angel talking to me. The angel will tell me what I need to know about the person. For instance, I was giving an angel reading to a woman and talking with her deceased husband. He said very loudly to her, "You need to rotate your tires!" When I relayed this message to the woman, she laughed. "I heard him say that to me just yesterday," she said, explaining that her car had been wobbling. I encouraged her to follow his advice without delay.

Clearing the Ear Chakras

Each of our psychic senses has a corresponding energy center—or *chakra*—devoted to it. Just as our eyes help us to see physically, so does our third-eye chakra help us to see spiritually. In the same way, our physical ears help us to hear earthly sounds, and our ear chakras help us to hear unearthly sounds.

Our ear chakras are located above our eyebrows. We have a left and a right ear chakra. They're slanted at an upward angle toward the center of our head. Think of Woody Allen's eyebrows as an example of the angle. These chakras spin (the word *chakra* means "wheel" in the ancient Eastern language, Sanskrit) at a fairly fast rate, so their movement casts a reddish-violet shade of energy.

We can hear clairaudiently much easier when our ear chakras are clean. Unfortunately, we get psychic debris in our ear chakras, and this clogs them as much as static on a telephone line would impair our ability to hear a caller.

Psychic debris collects in the ear chakras because of painful things that we hear. For instance, if we hear verbal abuse (from someone else, or self-directed), our ear chakras become wounded. They literally collapse from the weight of hearing abusive, angry, or violent words.

A very effective way to clear the ear chakras is to go outside on a sunny day and visualize the sun's rays clearing away the psychic dirt. In the absence of sunshine, toning aloud is also very helpful. Say some "Aum's" (the sacred sound of Creation) aloud, and concentrate on sending the vibrational energy to your ear chakras. Or, ring a crystal bowl or a brass chime, and put your ear chakras near the ringing sound.

But perhaps the most effective way to clear ear chakras is by releasing toxins toward abusive people in your life. Write a letter to that person (including one to yourself), and tell that person about all your feelings connected to verbal abuse. If you're angry, depressed, or fearful and you feel that it's related to being called names or hearing put-downs, write this in the letter. Then, tell the person that you're through being a victim. You're no longer going to accept anyone's version of reality but your own. You know that you're good person! You know that you're made in God's image and likeness, and that God only creates beauty inside and out.

Ask your angels to help you release the toxins of anger that remain in your heart, mind, and ear chakras. Then, take the letter and release it, either through burning it, drowning it in water, or freezing it. Don't send it to the person; this is a method that is private, and meant for you and your angels alone.

Noise Sensitivity

It's a good idea to clear your ear chakras once or twice a month, or whenever your spiritual hearing seems to be blocked. After your ear chakras are cleaned, you'll probably be more sensitive to noise. Ordinary noises may irritate you more than before, and you may find yourself covering your ears in response to sounds. You also may crave (and hopefully, create!) moments of silence. This could mean going to a remote location in nature, going on a formal silent retreat, or simply soaking in a bubble bath with a Do Not Disturb sign on the door.

Before you decide that it's too much hassle to deal with clean ear chakras, though, this increased sensitivity has definite benefits. You'll more easily hear your angels' whispers; as well as the sweet, soft voice of the Inner Presence. You will also have ready access to answers and guidance to any question. And, you'll be more inclined to understand that you're not alone.

The angels are always with us, and with the help of clean ear chakras, you'll be able to hear their messages clearly. You may also want to *feel* their presence, a topic that we'll touch on in the next chapter.

$$\text{❯❮ ❯❮ ❯❮}$$

CHAPTER EIGHTEEN

Feeling: Keys to Clairsentience

One of the most common ways in which we receive angelic communication and have contact with our angels is through our feelings. This process is called "clairsentience," or "clear feeling." Most people can relate to the experience of having a "gut feeling" or an intuitive sense. These are examples of the kinesthetic ways in which heaven communicates with us.

Denied Feelings

Most of my psychic-development students are aware of their clairsentience. So, the trouble isn't so much in opening this psychic channel. Rather, the area where most people are lacking with respect to clairsentience is in *trusting* these feelings. Eighty percent of my readings involve my validating what my client already suspects is true: "Yes, your mother is watching over you like an angel." "This business decision isn't quite ripe yet. You need more information." "Yes, this does look like it will develop into a long-term love relationship leading to marriage."

"That's what I felt!" my client exclaims with delight. While I'm happy to provide a second opinion to confirm my clients' feelings, I wish that more people would just trust their own feelings in the first place. We all tend to downplay and discount them way too much. "It's just a feeling," is a common example of the way we negate our emotions.

It may be a feeling, but that doesn't make it any less valid than if God and the angels spoke through a voice or a vision. For example, a woman named Jennifer Lulay Christianson was very happy that she listened to her feelings on a fateful day a couple of years ago:

Jennifer works at a television station in Portland, Oregon. Every afternoon for the past several years, she has routinely gone out the back door of the studio, gotten in her car, and driven home to her husband and young daughter. However, on this one particular day, Jennifer got a strong sense *not* to exit through that door. The feeling tugged at her to leave via the studio's front door instead. Furthermore, she felt a strong pull to find the nearest male co-worker and have him walk her out the front. What would *you* have done? Do you think that you would have obeyed or ignored this feeling?

Well, Jennifer complied. Although it was a long distance to the front door, she made the trek. Then, she asked the first man that she saw if he would escort her to her car. As soon as they exited, a loud sound thundered around them. Jennifer didn't know what the sound was, but the man, who just "happened" to be a Vietnam War veteran, recognized the sound of gunfire. He pushed Jennifer down and said, "Hit the deck!"

They crawled on their bellies, back into the studio. The receptionist met them and said, "Oh my gosh! There's a sniper with an automatic weapon shooting in the back parking lot." Jennifer gasped. She knew that if she hadn't listened to her feelings, she would have gone out that back door into the parking lot, and straight into the line of fire.

Jennifer related her story to me for this book, and asked that we think of what happened to her whenever we're tempted to ignore our feelings.

Overwhelming Feelings

For other people, though, the problem isn't denying feelings. It's overwhelming feelings. "I can't be around crowds at all!" said Susan, a psychic-development student. "I can feel every emotion of other people, and it drives me crazy." People like Susan who are super-sensitive feel bombarded with sensations from others.

Professional helpers—especially those who touch people for a living (massage therapists, cosmetologists, energy workers, and so on.), often absorb their clients' toxic energies. Counselors, nurses, teachers, and the like who listen to people's troubles all day sometimes become psychic sponges who soak up others' negativity. The result? Irritability, lethargy, and addictions.

If you're an ultrasensitive person, you may have been teased for being "too sensitive," but please don't close down your feelings as a result! This sensitivity is a gift. However, you may need to take steps to clear, shield, and protect yourself psychically.

Psychic Clearing, Shielding, and Protection

The angels say that sensitive people need to spend time in nature on a daily basis. Plants not only transmute carbon monoxide into oxygen, but they also clear away psychic dirt. It's very important for helping professionals and ultra-sensitive people to have lots of plants in their homes and offices. Please be sure that one or more of these plants are next to your bed. During the night, plants near your bed clear away any psychic dirt that you absorbed from clients or negative people (including yourself!).

Archangel Michael can clear away toxic energy in your mind, body, and heart. Simply close your eyes and say:

> *"Archangel Michael, I call upon you now. Please cut the cords that are draining me of energy and vitality. Thank you."*

Breathe deeply several times, and remain quiet while Michael and the other clearing angels complete their work. When your body feels settled, say:

> *"Archangel Michael, please clear away all negative energy I may have absorbed from my own thoughts and those of others."*

As before, remain quiet, and breathe deeply while your angelic healing transpires. It's a good idea to do this nightly, or whenever you're feeling inordinately tired or depressed.

To shield yourself from absorbing additional psychic dirt, here is a powerful method recently taught to me by the angels:

> Visualize a tall tube of pink light surrounding you. This pink light is a living, breathing, and very powerful being. It sends loving energy inwardly toward you, and also sends love outwardly toward others. So, you're protected, but not isolated, from other people. Your shield is sending them, as well as you, some nurturing energy. As a result, you won't feel the guilt normally associated with sealing yourself behind the armor of white light. The pink shield allows you to be warm and compassionate with

others, while shielding you from their negative thinking. If your lover or spouse is in a negative mood, surround yourself with this pink light before falling asleep together.

Ultrasensitive people feel better when they avoid hordes of people. So, plan your shopping trips, driving schedule, and movie-watching times so that you'll avoid large crowds. If you do find yourself in a large group, please use the pink shield described above.

Grounding

Sometimes people who are clairsentient feel disconnected from their bodies, as if they're living in a surreal dream, floating apart from their physical self. In such cases, it's important to ground yourself before you drive a car or operate other types of heavy machinery! Grounding also helps us appreciate each moment with our friends, family, nature, and other Earthly delights.

Some people use visualization techniques to ground themselves, such as picturing a tree root extending from the bottom of their feet, deep into the earth. Imagine drinking white-light energy upward through your roots, into your body. At the same time, imagine expelling any negative energy downward through your roots so that Mother Earth can heal and transmute the energy.

I prefer to ground myself by literally rooting myself into the earth. I take off my shoes and move my toes and soles upon soil, grass, sand, or water. I focus on the sensations in my feet and toes. Connecting with nature with bare feet is fun, healthful, and rapidly returns me to a greater awareness of my surroundings.

The angels also taught me to eat root foods—potatoes, yams, or carrots—as a grounding method. Eating a raw, organic carrot is probably one of the best grounding techniques I've ever used. A student of my Angel Therapy Practitioner certification course named Theresa approached me following a class one day. She and the students had spent eight hours practicing giving and receiving angel readings, and it was normal for them to feel a little tired and spacey afterward.

"I feel like I'm out of my body," Theresa told me. Since our class was held at an oceanfront hotel, I asked her to go outside and take a walk along the sand.

"Please be sure to eat some raw carrots, too," I added.

Michael, another student, gasped when he overheard me say this. He pulled out a plastic bag filled with cut carrots. "I was guided to bring these with me to class today!" he exclaimed. "I had no idea why, because I usually don't eat raw carrots. I just followed the guidance. Now I know that I brought them for you, Theresa. Here you go. They're even organic!"

Theresa told us the next morning that the combination of the carrots and the nature walk had immediately re-situated her center of awareness back into her body.

Common Clairsentient Occurrences

Most people have had a clairsentient experience. Gut or intuitive feelings are probably the most common example. Many times, this is how God and the angels speak to us. For instance, your deceased loved one may warn you to change lanes while driving, and you receive the message as a feeling that tugs at you.

But there are also more profound ways to experience clairsentience, including the following:

- *Wings brushing against you.* Feeling someone or something touch, or move across, your skin or hair. It's not as creepy as it sounds. Almost everyone I've interviewed says the experience is extremely pleasant and makes them feel loved.

- *Feeling someone sit down on your bed.* You feel a person sitting beside you, and you swear that you can even see the indents in the bedspread. Or, you're sitting on the sofa, and you feel your deceased dog or cat jump onto the seat beside you.

- *Sensing a particular person's presence.* We're all psychic mediums with varying degrees of sensitivity and faith in our abilities. When you sense that a particular deceased loved one is with you, chances are that you're correct. Each person has a unique energy "fingerprint," and we can sense which loved one entered the room, and whether that loved one is deceased or living.

- *Feeling your ear pinched.* Very often, our spirit guides pull our earlobes as a way of goading us along. If this sensation is ever painful, please tell your spirit guide to find a gentler way to lead you on the path.

- *Someone tucking you in.* You're having a difficult time sleeping, but then you feel a comforting presence beside you. You know that it's your guardian angel or a departed loved one. The next thing you know, you have blankets pulled over you, and you're tucked in. Feeling very safe, comfortable, and loved, you drift peacefully off to sleep.

- *Air pressure and temperature changes.* As if you've changed altitudes, the air thickens or thins. You realize that this air-pressure change is from a being entering your presence. Or, the room temperature suddenly drops or soars. Unlike the movie *The Sixth Sense*, which implied that spirit guides only created a chilly room, an *increase* in room temperature can also signify that a deceased loved one or additional angels have entered the room. I always ask my psychic-development students to dress in layers, because the room temperature peaks and plummets throughout the day as we invoke angels and loved ones.

- *Stomach or jaw sensations.* You enter a roomful of people and your stomach tightens. As you think about the new job that has just been offered to you, your jaw clenches. Signs of tension? Of course. But ask yourself: Why am I feeling tension in connection to this situation? It could be that your angels are trying to caution you. Often, our body is aware of the truth before our conscious mind admits it. The body acts like a divining instrument that ferrets out whether something or someone is in integrity or not.

- *Sudden pain or illness.* You feel fine, your health is good, and you've been treating your body with care. But then you suddenly have an attack of pain or illness from out of nowhere. It feels like you've been ambushed. Well, chances are that you *have* been. When another person is angry with you, studies show that your heart rate and blood pressure increase. If that person's fury continues, your body may feel the psychic attack and translate it into a sharp pain (like a sword has stabbed you) or an illness (because the other person's anger is making you sick). You can use the psychic clearing and protection methods described earlier in this chapter to shield yourself from psychic attack, and heal any attack that has already occurred.

- *Sensing that something's off, or just not right.* Someone invites you to participate in a business venture. It's the opportunity you've been waiting for, but something feels off about the deal. You decide against participating, and a year later, you read that those who did participate are suing for fraud.

  Similarly, you're sitting at home and suddenly get an eerie feeling that your child is in trouble. You get a call an hour later that he's been in a car accident. Fortunately, no one, including your child, was injured.

- *Smelling flowers, perfume, smoke, or some other disembodied scent.* You smell your deceased grandmother's cologne, or your late father's cigar smoke. These are signs that this particular loved one is with you. Or, you smell flowers from out of nowhere. Usually, flowers are a sign that the winged angels are validating their nearness to you. Sometimes the smell of roses is a signal that Mother Mary is with you. She is a loving, nondenominational ascended master who comes to anyone who calls upon her. She also comes to people whose life purpose involves helping children.

- *Psychic lovemaking.* You're a female in bed, and you feel the energy of a male spirit hovering near you. You suddenly feel sensations of romance and passion, and you realize that the male spirit is making gestures of foreplay. Then you let go, and you allow the spirit to make love to you. In many ways, the sensations are just as pleasurable (if not more so) as a physical companion. If the spirit is your late boyfriend or husband, this episode is one of high spiritual frequency. However, many earthbound spirits (deceased people with a lower ego consciousness) look for willing living females with whom to make love. They never rape anyone; you must consent to make love.

  So, please be careful when allowing a spirit to engage sexually with you. If you sense that it's a deceased lover, you can trust this feeling. But if you don't know the identity of the lover, I would certainly insist they go away. I would call upon Archangel Michael to make sure this tomcat never returned to my environment. If you've made love to such a spirit in the past, just put it behind you, and make a vow to only share your body with lovers of the highest spiritual caliber from now on.

Awakening Your Clairsentience

Did you read the previous descriptions and feel that you've been missing something? That you would love to be more aware of your intuition, or feel emotions more deeply? Well, you *can* increase your clairsentient sensitivity—with some practice.

Each form of psychic guidance is associated with a particular chakra, as we've discussed. For instance:

Clairvoyance (seeing) is regulated by the third eye, or brow, chakra. *Clairaudience* (hearing) is associated with the ear chakras. *Clairsentience* (feeling) stems from the heart chakra. So, the key to increasing your clairsentience is through opening the heart chakra. You can increase all these areas of psychic receptivity by paying attention to all three chakras.

To open your heart chakra, and thus your clairsentience, you need to allow yourself to feel more deeply. This represents a risk, of course, of feeling some painful emotions—not from our angels, but from our own ego. As you know, some people shut down their heart and accept blunted emotions in exchange for a guarantee of not feeling emotional pain. However, by doing so, they also deny themselves wonderful emotions such as deep love, playful joy, and spiritual bliss.

If a person has been traumatically hurt—by child abuse, for example—they may have developed emotionally painful patterns in their life, such as becoming involved with abusive "friends" or lovers.

When we clear the hurt from the past and decide to open our heart chakras, we can break those patterns. They're a tragic irony, in that we unconsciously replicate emotional trauma—usually by seeking out situations or people that mirror the original unpleasantness.

In addition, your open heart acts like a screener who will tell you if a potential new lover, friend, or business associate has integrity or not. So, by opening your heart, you actually ensure your emotional *safety* in relationships. That's because you'll more easily "hear" feedback from your heart when it's open.

Clearing and Opening the Heart

Sometimes a history of child abuse requires intense treatment from loving mental-health professionals. If you decide to seek counseling, be sure that you choose a therapist who is experienced (or better yet, who specializes) in treating child-abuse issues.

I'm also very impressed by the new body-oriented treatment methods for trauma survivors. Many well-documented studies show that Eye Movement Desensitization and Reprocessing (EMDR) and Somatic Experiencing (S.E.) help trauma survivors rapidly heal from posttraumatic stress disorder. Both types of treatment are administered by trained therapists. You can find more information and local treatment professionals for EMDR on the Website [**www. emdria. com**]; and for S.E., on the Website [**www.fhe.com**].

What is traumatic to one person might be less painful to the next. Everyone has experienced disappointment and hurt in their lives. Some people are able to heal emotional wounds using spiritual methods without requiring a professional's assistance. But getting professional help isn't a sign of weakness or being "less than." It can actually be a sign of strength to ask for help.

In my book *Healing with the Fairies* (Hay House, 2001), I wrote about the importance of clearing the wounds of our past so that we can more clearly manifest our future. Whenever we affirm or visualize an intention, we're painting a picture on our heart of what we desire. If our heart is heavy with unhealed emotional wounds, it's as if we're painting that new picture on a dirty canvas. The old pictures (from past wounds) will bleed through the new painting and cause distortion when we manifest.

That's another reason why clearing and opening the heart is essential. In *Healing with the Fairies*, I discussed how being outside in nature can help us heal and open our hearts. In particular, sit beneath a tree by yourself. Mentally "tell" that tree about your past emotional wounds, and imagine "giving" those situations and the accompanying pain to the tree spirit. Although this may sound like a far-out method, it is actually ancient, powerful, and effective. The trees have a loving, stable energy that helps us feel safe and cared for.

In addition, ancient wisdom holds that the aroma and essential oil of pink roses helps us to open our heart chakras. Buy yourself a present of at least one pink rose, or plant a pink rosebush in your yard, and drink in the fragrance frequently. I also love the essential oil of roses, particularly from a company called Young Living Essential Oils. You simply breathe in this aroma, and you can feel it opening and warming your heart chakra. More information about these oils is on the company's Website: [**www.youngliving.com**].

Another way to open the heart is through yoga. Many of the yoga postures, or *asanas*, stretch the chest and rib areas. The movements and inner focusing have profound chakra-opening effects, especially the heart chakra. I also find that yoga is a wonderful way for busy or stressed-out people to meditate. If you've felt guided to attend yoga classes, I highly recommend giving it a try. It's normal to feel intimidated at first, or to think you're too busy to attend. But just start with a gentle class at a studio near your home, or follow along with a yoga video-cassette. I think you'll be glad you did!

Here's another wonderful way to clear and open the heart chakra: Imagine that an ascended master (such as Jesus, a saint, Quan Yin, etc.) or a guardian angel is standing in front of you. Now, see or feel yourself sending a stream of love energy from your heart to theirs. Notice what happens next. Almost immediately, this great, heavenly being will return the love to your heart, magnified by 100 percent. As if the light that you've sent is bouncing off a mirror, you'll feel your heart bathed in powerful Divine love.

My *Chakra Clearing* audiotape (Hay House, 1997) is also very effective for opening the heart and other chakras. During the heart chakra-opening portion of the tape, Archangel Michael helps you lose the fear of being loved, and of giving love. The angels say that these fears of love keep us from fully experiencing the joy and power of our spiritual gifts.

Tuning in and Trusting

We can also increase our awareness of clairsentient messages by practicing "body awareness." Sometimes lightworkers dissociate from their own bodies, and they aren't aware of their physical selves. To get a balance of being aware of spirit while walking in the flesh, we can practice tuning in to our physical sensations.

For instance, how comfortable are you right now? Spend a moment focusing your awareness on your bottom, back, and legs. Are they comfortable? How about your shoes, underwear, and clothing? How do they feel? Is the room stuffy, hot, or cold? If anything is uncomfortable, spend a moment adjusting your position, changing the room temperature, opening a window, or removing binding clothing.

The most important part of developing clairsentience, however, is learning to *trust your feelings*. Yet, every time we ignore our feelings, we learn to trust them more. For instance, have you ever become involved with a person when you had a strong feeling that you shouldn't? These situations teach us to listen the next time, don't they?

One way to develop more self-trust is by keeping a "Psychic Journal." It's best to use a pocket- or purse-sized notebook so that it's handy for making quick notes. Make an entry every time you have a strong or unusual feeling, such as an impression about a co-worker, an intuition about which route to drive to work, or a gut feeling about a new acquaintance. Write the date next to each entry. Then, review the journal on a regular basis. You'll find that many of your feelings become validated by future events. This will help you develop more confidence in your feelings so that you'll be more apt to trust—and follow—them.

ЭЄ ЭЄ ЭЄ

AFTERWORD

Y ou already connect with your angels in many wonderful ways, including the dreams, feelings, and signs that you receive. Reading angel stories also tends to increase our awareness of the presence of angels in our lives. So, just the process of reading this book will likely create an angel experience, of which you'll be consciously aware.

I find that our emotional climate can either breed or block angel connections. When we have an extremely strong emotion—such as fear, anger, or worry—and we simultaneously appeal for heaven's help, this often triggers an angel experience. However, if we have these strong emotions and *don't* ask for help, we can actually block ourselves from hearing their guidance. So, asking is the essential key.

You can request help from God, Holy Spirit, Jesus (or other ascended masters), the archangels, your guardian angel, or deceased loved ones in so many different ways:

- ***Think the thought, "Help me!"*** Heaven hears our thoughts, and responds with assistance.

- ***Speak your request aloud.*** The words you choose, and the way that you say them, are unimportant. What counts is sincerity.

- *Write a letter to heaven.* Pour your heart out, including all your fears, worries, and hopes. Again, don't worry about being "proper." They're angels, not English teachers.

- *Invite them into your dreams.* Before falling asleep, pray to have a connection with your angels. Invite them (or a particular being in heaven) into your dreams. It's also helpful to write down your prayer and place the piece of paper under your pillow.

- *Ask for a sign.* Ask your angels to make their presence known through one of the ways discussed in the angel stories, and in the chapters on clairvoyance, clairaudience, and clairsentience. Don't specify how you want the sign to appear—let the angels surprise you with their method. But *do* ask the angels to make it a very clear sign that you won't overlook.

- *Ask for faith.* If you find yourself filled with self-doubt, ask your angels to boost your spiritual confidence. Even if you're unsure whether you have angels, or whether they really exist, ask anyway. The easiest way is to mentally speak to your angels before falling asleep. Appeal to them to buoy your faith, and to connect with you so that you're sure of their presence.

You *are* surrounded by angels, right now. Even if you're a nonbeliever, you have guardian angels who love you, and who are with you, at this very moment. Close your eyes for a moment, breathe deeply, and feel their presence. If you still can't sense the angels, keep going. The angels are even more motivated to make their presence known than you are. They love you so much, and want to become more involved in your life.

Imagine for a moment what it must be like to be your guardian angel. Do you think it's a stressful or frustrating job? Our angels' purpose is to help bring peace upon Earth, one person at a time. When we ask our angels for help, and allow them to help us, we're helping the angels to fulfill their missions.

When my guardian angel saved my life during an armed carjacking in July of 1995, I learned a very important lesson: God could send angels to help save my life, but it was up to *me* to accept that help. The angels had warned me that my car would be stolen that day unless I put the top up on my convertible. I ignored this warning, and it almost cost me my life. Fortunately, during the carjacking, the angels gave me a second chance. They told me to scream with all my might! This time I listened!

My life was spared because I *allowed* God and the angels to help me. That moment changed my life forever. I now know the importance of asking the angels for help, and then following their guidance when it comes. This may be one of the most important positive habits that we can develop.

Connecting with your angels, then, is much more than a personal growth venture. It's a relationship that helps us to remember and work on our Divine life purpose, and to enact God's plan of peace. It's a relationship that could make a life-and-death difference for ourselves and our loved ones.

Our relationship with God, the ascended masters, our angels, and deceased loved ones can ultimately help us love ourselves and others more deeply. By opening our heart to heaven, we literally open our heart to life itself. In that way, we can all become Earth Angels.

ॐ ॐ ॐ

About the Author

Doreen Virtue, Ph.D., is a clairvoyant doctor of psychology who works with the angelic and elemental realms. She is the author of numerous books, tapes, and oracle cards, including *Healing with the Angels, Angel Therapy*, and *Divine Guidance*. A frequent guest on television and radio talk shows, Doreen is often referred to as "The Angel Lady."

Doreen gives workshops each weekend on topics related to her books. For information, please visit her Website: **www.AngelTherapy.com**

❦❦❦

Hay House Titles of Related Interest

Books

Ask and It Is Given, *Learning to Manifest Your Desires,*
by Esther and Jerry Hicks

Faeriecraft, by Alicen and Neil Geddes-Ward

God, Creation, and Tools for Life, by Sylvia Browne

The Indigo Children: *The New Kids Have Arrived,*
by Lee Carroll and Jan Tober

Through My Eyes, by Gordon Smith

CDs

10 Secrets for Success and Inner Peace, by Wayne W. Dyer

101 Power Thoughts, by Louise L. Hay

Angels, Guides and Ghosts, by Sylvia Browne

Developing Your Own Psychic Powers, by John Edward

HAY HOUSE PUBLISHERS

We hope you enjoyed this Hay House book.
If you would like to receive a free catalogue featuring additional
Hay House books and products, or if you would like information
about the Hay Foundation, please contact:

Hay House UK Ltd

292B Kensal Rd • London W10 5BE
Tel: (44) 20 8962 1230; Fax: (44) 20 8962 1239
www.hayhouse.co.uk

***

Published and distributed in the United States of America by:
Hay House, Inc. • PO Box 5100 • Carlsbad, CA 92018-5100
Tel: (1) 760 431 7695 or (800) 654 5126;
Fax: (1) 760 431 6948 or (800) 650 5115
www.hayhouse.com

Published and distributed in Australia by:
Hay House Australia Ltd • 18/36 Ralph St • Alexandria NSW 2015
Tel: (61) 2 9669 4299 • Fax: (61) 2 9669 4144
www.hayhouse.com.au

Published and distributed in the Republic of South Africa by:
Hay House SA (Pty) Ltd • PO Box 990 • Witkoppen 2068
Tel/Fax: (27) 11 706 6612 • orders@psdprom.co.za

Distributed in Canada by:
Raincoast • 9050 Shaughnessy St • Vancouver, BC V6P 6E5
Tel: (1) 604 323 7100 • Fax: (1) 604 323 2600

***

Sign up via the Hay House UK website to receive the Hay House
online newsletter and stay informed about what's going on with
your favourite authors. You'll receive bimonthly announcements
about discounts and offers, special events, product highlights,
free excerpts, giveaways, and more!
www.hayhouse.co.uk